MW01616512

Be A Leader for God's Sake -- From values to behaviors

A revision of the 1997 edition of Be a Manager for God's Sake.

Bruce E. Winston, Ph.D.

Connie
2 Tim 3:16
Enjoy the journey

Production and distribution by:
School of Leadership Studies
Regent University
1000 Regent University Drive
Virginia Beach, VA 23464

ISBN 0-9725819-0-1

Single copies of this book may be purchased at www.amazon.com and selected bookstores.

Orders for 10 or more books may be ordered at a distributor price from:
School of Leadership Studies
Regent University
1000 Regent University Drive
Virginia Beach, VA 23464
757-226-4306

Content used in this book is also found in the seminar Be a Leader for God's Sake® presented by Bruce E. Winston, Ph.D. For more information on the seminar please contact Bruce Winston at the address above. A four-videotape set of the seminar Be a Leader for God's Sake® is available as well.

Preface to the Revised Edition

In my early days of teaching in the Regent University School of Business MBA program, roughly 1994-96, it was difficult to find books or articles that explained the scriptural base of leadership, or at least leadership as I saw it represented in the Scriptures. To answer this need, I began writing essays to help the MBA students better understand what the Bible has to say about managing and leading people. In 1998, the School of Business published a collection of these essays in a book called Be a Manager for God's Sake.

Since that first publication, I have transferred to the School of Leadership Studies at Regent University and have shifted the focus of my teaching to training leaders in all types of organizations rather than just training leaders in business.

My new focus on training organizational leaders, in America and literally around the world (thanks to the Internet), has brought me to the crossroads of revising my book. This second edition contains stories from my own experience of seeking to *Be a Leader for God's Sake*. It is my sincere hope that the message of this book will take you closer to understanding how you become the leader you were intended to be, a leader for God's sake.

This new phase of my own journey has encouraged some re-thinking on my part. I have come to understand that leadership is leadership -- regardless of the type of company or organization. I won't be surprised if some folks have a little trouble with this notion, in fact, in my early days with the School of Leadership Studies, I had believed that the leaders of schools, churches, para-church ministries, and commercial enterprises were all different. But as I continued to work with these master's and doctoral students who were leaders from all types of organizations, it became clear that regardless of the types of situations they were in, they each faced the same types of problems and challenges. Amazingly, they all shared the same, basic foundational values of leadership. Even with the differences between the various disciplines and cultures, the core terminology, values and semantics apply.

I have presented numerous seminars based on this content and participants have aided in the process of proving this theory. Learning from their astute questions, I could see how the leader's foundational <u>values</u> yield <u>beliefs,</u> and how their beliefs yield <u>intentions to behave</u>, and how from their intentions spring actual <u>behavior</u>. The leader's behavior then helps form the followers' <u>attitudes</u> that <u>affect</u> how followers behave. These steps form the path of this book: (1) foundational values, (2) how values relate to behaviors, (3) how leaders interact with the organization, and (4) how followers interact with leaders. Since it is impossible to completely separate each of these elements, the chapters of this book include each of the four elements.

During this time of my own journey through the process of internalizing the values of the Beatitudes, I read the book *Flight of the Buffalo* by James Belasco, and I identified with his imagery of the leader who saw himself as a buffalo that wanted to transform himself into an eagle and soar above the earth.

As the buffalo worked at transforming himself, he would achieve the state of the eagle from time to time only to find that while he was an eagle, he would revert to his buffalo values and tactics and turn back into a buffalo and crash to the ground. I described this book to my staff and committed myself to continue to work on the transformation, and asked the employees who worked with me, if they would also commit to reminding me when I became the buffalo again.

Note to the fourth printing:

My thanks to Jane Waddell for her proofreading and suggested edits to the book. The product is better now because of her efforts.

- Foundational Values
- Values Relate to behavior
- Leaders Interact w Org.
- Followers Interact w leaders

Dedication

I am indebted to the many students and seminar attendees who have tested my understanding of these concepts and who have helped me shape my understanding through our many dialogues. I am also grateful to Julia Matera and Kerry Park who read and edited this current edition. I want to recognize the contribution of Julianne Robbins Cenac who helped me work through the original essays on the Fruit of the Spirit and Proverbs 31.

I am especially grateful to my wife and friend Kristie who has traveled many miles with me on numerous seminars setting up equipment, handing out materials, and helping me see what content areas the audience might like more information about.

Bruce E. Winston, Ph.D.

Table of Contents

Introduction

At last count, there were over 10,000 articles and books on leadership that have emerged in the last few years. A recent query at www.amazon.com on the word leadership produced 8,616 hits. So why write another book on leadership? What is it about this book that is different? The answer lies in the simplicity of leadership itself -- that leadership starts with values. Many of the books currently on the market attempt to define the behaviors of leaders, or at least in the minds of the authors, the most important behaviors. Leaders read the material and attempt to practice the behaviors -- usually with mixed results. My approach focuses first on the values of leadership as described in The Beatitudes found in Matthew 5:3-11, and then proceeds to discuss the behaviors that follow The Beatitudes (Matthew 5:13 - 7:27).

To help the reader use this information, I have included short pause and reflect sections throughout this edition. These pause and reflect points are the same as what the psalmist meant with the word *Selah* found in many of the songs and poems in the Book of Psalms.

The first premise of this book is that values have to be based on something, and that *"something"* for this book, is *agapao* love as presented in the first chapter. This concept supports my theory that leadership begins with this overarching value of love that forms the foundation for the other lesser values.

The second premise of this book is that human leaders are just human! We are not perfect, and most of us, myself included, fail in our efforts to live the life of a perfect leader. A key to preventing followers from becoming disenchanted with their leader(s) is for the leader to admit a lack of perfection, and to do so frequently! Followers can be very

1

forgiving if they see their leader(s) admitting faults and continually trying to improve.

As you read this book, take time at the *Selah* sections and make some notes to yourself about what values you need to work on. If you are comfortable that you have your values in place, then start by thinking about the behaviors that emerge from the values. Spend some time with a few followers who are willing to tell you the truth as they see you! Good leaders are accountable to their followers, and this accountability is one of the traits of leaders who follow the concepts laid out in this book.

Every author brings his or her biases and beliefs to the manuscript, and I offer mine up front. I am not a biblical scholar, so I am grateful for the opportunity to work at Regent University where we do have biblical scholars who have reviewed my work at various stages of the manuscript. I am a leader who approaches Scripture-seeking in order to understand how the words recorded so long ago, apply to today's world of organizations and leaders. For many of us, the situations presented in the Old and New Testaments are difficult to comprehend since there is little direct relation to situations today. For example, salt was a precious and rare element to the Hebrews living in Israel at the time of the Sermon on the Mount. Today, however, we have plenty of salt, so much in fact that we take it for granted. These differences alone would be enough to complicate our understanding of Scripture, but we also face the challenge of the translation of the Word from the original Greek into English. While English is a wonderful language -- and thankfully for us in the United States, it is a commonly used language around the world -- it is not a good language to use for translating Biblical Greek. Biblical Greek is a very

--- Mark 12:33

"But I tell you who hear me: <u>Love</u> your enemies, do good to those who hate you, . . ."

--- Luke 6:27

"If you <u>love</u> those who <u>love</u> you, what credit is that to you? Even 'sinners' <u>love</u> those who <u>love</u> them."

--- Luke 6:32

"But <u>love</u> your enemies, do good to them, and lend to them without expecting to get anything back. Then your reward will be great, and you will be sons of the Most High, because he is kind to the ungrateful and wicked."

--- Luke 6:35

"No servant can serve two masters. Either he will hate the one and <u>love</u> the other, or he will be devoted to the one and despise the other. You cannot serve both God and Money."

--- Luke 16:13

"Jesus said to them, 'If God were your Father, you would <u>love</u> me, for I came from God and now am here. I have not come on my own; but he sent me.'"

--- John 8:42

"So the sisters sent word to Jesus, 'Lord, the one you <u>love</u> is sick.'"

--- John 11:3

"A new command I give you: <u>Love</u> one another. As I have <u>loved</u> you, so you must <u>love</u> one another."

--- John 13:34

"If you <u>love</u> me, you will obey what I command."

--- John 14:15

"Whoever has my commands and obeys them, he is the one who <u>loves</u> me. He who <u>loves</u> me will be <u>loved</u> by my Father, and I too will <u>love</u> him and show myself to him."

--- John 14:21

"Jesus replied, 'If anyone <u>loves</u> me, he will obey my teaching. My Father will <u>love</u> him, and we will come to him and make our home with him.'"

--- John 14:23

"He who does not <u>love</u> me will not obey my teaching. These words you hear are not my own; they belong to the Father who sent me."

--- John 14:24

" . . . but the world must learn that I <u>love</u> the Father and that I do exactly what my Father has commanded me. 'Come now; let us leave.'"

--- John 14:31

Agapao love is alive and well today and may be best understood in light of the Golden Rule: *"Do unto others as you would have them do unto to you,"* and even more to the Platinum Rule of *"Do unto others as they want you to do unto them."* *Agapao*, as a moral love, means that today's leaders must consider the human and spiritual aspects of their employees/followers. The people working for you are not just flesh and blood who respond to wages as a mule responds to a carrot on a stick. Your employees are complete people with physical, mental, and spiritual needs.

Employees today do not see the employer through the same loyalty-shaded glasses, as did the employees of the 1950s. Rather, there is a much greater sense from employees that they stay with an employer because it is mutually beneficial on several levels: in physical terms, such as compensation; in mental terms, such as in a stimulating relationship; and in spiritual terms, such that the greater "self" is served and blessed by the involvement with the leader. This is the basis for love (*agapao*), to consider each employee/follower as a total person with needs, wants, and desires. Employees want to be considered for their brains and their hearts as well as their hands. The call of *agapao* love in the organization is to go far beyond seeing people as "hired hands," to seeing them as "hired hearts."

You may be surprised to find that God calls leaders to love more than their employees. Employees and followers want leaders who are honest, open, and who keep the organization moving in a positive direction during both calm and stormy seas. Employees and followers want leaders who are "others-centered." Employees and followers want leaders who can bring out the best qualities in them. This requires leadership -- *agapao* leadership! Beyond this, leaders must also love all the organization's stakeholders from customers, vendors, regulators, shareholders, members, as well as contributors.

In his book, Leadership Jazz, Max Depree provides a wonderful and colorful description of the employer/employee exchanges that happen in servant leadership. I believe his metaphor also applies to *agapao* leadership.

> "A Jazz band is an expression of servant leadership. The leader of a jazz band has the beautiful opportunity to draw the best out of the other musicians. We have much to learn from jazz-band leaders. For jazz, like leadership, combines the unpredictability of the future with the gifts of individuals" (p. 9).

Depree is saying that you must love someone so much that, within the framework of employment, you care enough to learn the gifts of the individual and draw out from them what is good and what fits the needs of the organization. This focus puts the emphasis on the employee first followed by learning what the individual's "best" talents are, and then seeking how to apply this to the organization. People who engage their gifts and work in the areas of their abilities are happier and more productive. The simplicity of this is obvious when you consider that employees who are happy produce more and with less effort. The end result is better for the organization. However, the *agapao* leader must not see the employee as just a benefit to the organization, but must also see the reciprocal benefit to the employee.

The paradox of an *agapao* form of leadership, compared to an economic form of leadership, is that while the *agapao* leader concentrates less on the organization and more on individuals the organization gains more because the employees are working to uphold the organization's needs.

Here's a personal example of this relationship in action. Some of the employees with whom I work have young children. From time to time, an employee's child will get sick or need additional care that results in the employee missing work. From an economic view of leadership, it doesn't make sense to encourage parents, moms or dads, to stay home and provide the extra childcare needed. But, in an *agapao* form of leadership, we encourage the employee to stay home. My experience so far, is that every employee who has an *agapao* view of the leader-follower relationship has accomplished more work, even with the occasional days spent at home. How does this happen? It's simple. The employee arranges to take work home with them or arranges for the spouse to pick up materials on his or her way home in the evening, or the employee takes work home over the next couple of days, or comes in on the weekend to accomplish the needed tasks. *Agapao* behavior is a relationship and the behavior is reciprocal. Also, since the employee knows that the *agapao* leader has the employee's best interest at heart, the employee is willing to go the extra mile for the leader.

> *"Every great man is always being helped by everybody; for his gift is to get good out of all things and all persons."*
> *--John Ruskin*

Although there are short-term elements of the leader-follower relationship, such as financial compensation, for the *agapao* leadership paradigm to be successful, the paradigm should be viewed as a long-term condition.

How did we become so unloving?

Taylor's scientific leadership concepts, that so many of us have practiced over the years, focuses on the pay part of the leader-employee relationship. In and of itself, there is nothing wrong with this. In the early 1900s, Taylor saw the poor conditions in which his employees lived and he longed to do something about it. He knew that he could not just give a raise to every worker since this violated his stewardship obligation to the owners of the steel mill where he worked (Weisbord, 1991).

Taylor knew that if he developed a better way for employees to produce more for the company, he could pass some of the increased reward to the employees. He was successful, and his employees earned more pay that led to better living conditions for the workers' families. Taylor clearly desired to meet the physical needs of his employees. However, Taylor fell short in two areas as he ignored the emotional and spiritual needs of the employees.

In the 1930s, the human behavior school of thought promulgated by Mayo, McGregor, and Argyris, among others, emphasized the emotional and social side of employees. These theories led to a *phileo* love where leaders strove to meet the emotional needs of the employee.

The human resource school of thought followed the human behavior school of thought and taught leaders to treat people as bearers of skills and abilities. This concept advocates the hiring of the whole person, not just a jobholder. This progression brought us closer to treating the employee as a whole person body, mind, and soul, and this is the state to which DePree referred.

Unfortunately, not all leaders followed the progression from the scientific school to the human resource school. It seems that for many leaders, the scientific school was the last classroom that they attended. Of course, this is reasonable since the main focus of the commercial enterprise community has been on Adam Smith's concepts of self-love

Taylor: Economic

McGregor-Argyrin. Phileo

H.R School of Thought
DePree: whole person

12

Adam Smith: Self-love

as stated in his 1776 document, *The Wealth of Nations*. Smith wrote:

> *It is not from the benevolence of the butcher, the brewer, or the baker that we expect our dinner, but from their regard to their own interest. We address ourselves, not to their humanity but to their self-love, and never talk to them of our own necessities but of their advantages.*

In Smith's opinion, no one does anything except for what's in it for self. Unfortunately, our foundational concepts regarding commercial endeavors are based on Smith's writings. It is not surprising that we see so much self-love in our commercial enterprises and so little *agapao* love. A more thorough reading of Smith's *Wealth of Nations* reveals many other values and beliefs that have shaped our leader-follower values and relationships. For now, consider how Smith's statement creates a value of mistrust and caution when engaging other people. If suppliers are only interested in their own benefit, then it is logical that employees and leaders are also only interested in their own self-interests and that they will only engage in activities that are personally profitable. What a marked contrast to *agapao* leadership.

Another layer to the leader-follower relationship was created by the concept of functional supervision, a characteristic of the scientific school. This concept suggests that foremen in a company must be specialists in an area of a company's operation in order to lead the workers. Functional superiority led supervisors to believe that they were better than the workers and that workers should not think, but rather do what the supervisor required. While it is true that the functional foreman did know more about the subject matter, it did not imply that the foreman was better than the worker or that the worker should not think independently. Rather, the foreman became a repository of information available to others.

A similar scenario occurred with the administrative duties that supervisors once performed. In order to allow the supervisors to have more time to become functionally proficient, Taylor's approach to leadership removed the functions of record keeping, payroll, etc., and assigned these administrative functions to separate departments. Soon, the supervisors found people in support departments acting like they were better than the supervisors -- an interesting process of values, to beliefs, to attitudes, to behaviors! The values defined in The Beatitudes speak against both this self-love and self-aggrandizement.

How should we love?

Knowing that we should love our employees is not enough. We must understand how to love. Moral love begins with values. Some say that if you act a role long enough, you will become the role. I do not think this applies to this *agapao* type of love, because you have to think first.

Scripture says that what we think is as important as what we do (Matthew 5). Leaders must then think in morally loving terms toward employees before they act. Leaders who practice thinking in morally loving terms will find that actions soon follow. Sally Helgesen, in her book *The Female Advantage - Women's Ways of Leadership*, implies that women think about employees in a more loving manner than men. I believe women may be better at demonstrating moral love to others. At least, in retrospect, I recall more women leaders showing moral love or relational behaviors to employees than men.

What a loving world might be like

Utopia it is not. Comfortable it is not. Easy it is not. Wonderful it is! These are bold statements to make, I agree. When you love someone, that person doesn't always do as you wish. The other person sometimes makes mistakes, and though communication is never perfect, there is a sense of trust and acceptance that goes a long way to causing the relationship to improve. It is this acceptance-repentance-forgiveness-trust cycle that emerges from an *agapao* leadership style. But what about obstinate employees who just seem interested in their own gain? Clearly, there are people who do not want to enter into relationships. They just want a job. Usually this is a matter of being in the wrong organization or being in the wrong sub-organization of a larger organization. Sometimes this may be a matter of immaturity on the part of the employee. Wise leaders build trust in small increments and the employee's level of maturity will rise or fall with each occasion. The *agapao* leader seeks to increase the level of the employee's maturity before higher levels of trust are bestowed.

> *"You may be deceived if you trust too much, but you will live in torment if you don't trust enough."*
> *--Frank Crane*

I recall several employees, over the years, that appeared to be stubborn, inflexible, and unwilling to behave in an *agapao* manner. Ninety percent of the time the problems stemmed from the employees being in a position that did not match their gifts or abilities; having expectations that were too high relative to their self-perception of capability; or having a string of past work failures that resulted in strong defensive barrier intended to protect them from being hurt again. I recall one particular employee that suffered from several past work failures that resulted in the employee losing her self-esteem. To help this situation, I invested some time getting to know the employee, and even letting her fail a few times without repercussions. She began to realize that the workplace could be an emotionally safe environment and within a year, she was relaxed, hardworking, offered help to other employees, and began to offer suggestions for work-performance improvement in her own position. Sadly, not all employees are happy or can be helped to be happy. My estimate is that about 10 percent of the time a successful resolution can't be reached. Sometimes you'll be faced with a recalcitrant employee who does not want to consider the needs of the organization. If no relationship can occur, then it is best for the employee to be asked to leave. The termination will usually occur because of poor performance since few self-serving employees perform well in an *agapao* leadership environment. There are also environments where Smith and Taylor's values are strongly entrenched. In these situations, self-serving employees can perform well enough, but the end-result will be that employees will only meet their financial needs and most likely, will seek to professionally destroy others as they seek to improve their own lot.

Loving employees in a moral sense creates an environment in which people know that their intelligence and insights merit consideration.

> *"We seem to want mass production, but we must remember that men are individuals not to be satisfactorily dealt with in masses, and the making of men is more important than the production of things."*
> *--Ralph W. Sockman*

People operating in a spirit of *agapao* love do not always work diligently by themselves. People entering a loving work environment may even slow down and bask in the warmth and friendship that occurs in an *agapao*-led organization. However, the slow-down effect is often short-lived as the renewed pace of hard work that usually emerges more than compensates for the slow beginning. *Agapao* does not mean a reduction of pressure, but rather a sense of encouragement and support during times of difficulty and stress. Loving employees requires more of you as the leader because you must accept by faith that employees will complete work by deadlines.

> *"Gentleness is a divine trait: Nothing is so strong as gentleness, and nothing is so gentle as real strength."*
> *-- Ralph W. Sockman*

> *"You can employ men and hire hands to work for you. But you must win their hearts to have them work with you."*
> *-- Florio*

> *"To love means to commit oneself without guarantee, to give oneself completely in the hope that our love will produce love in the loved person. Love is an act of faith, and whoever is of little faith is also of little love."*
> *-- Erich Fromm*

Conclusion

Loving leaders treat employees as though they possess intelligence and creativity. Loving leaders give trust to employees. Please note that loving employees reciprocate with love and performance, and this is where I believe that

17

Adam Smith missed it. Relationships do not exist on a transactional basis solely, although there is always an element of transaction, relationships exist predominantly in the realm of transformation.

To be loved is to allow oneself to be used for the greater good of the other.

> *"Contentment, and indeed usefulness, comes as the infallible result of great acceptances, great humilities -- of not trying to make ourselves this or that, but of surrendering ourselves to the fullness of life -- of letting life flow through us. To be used - that is the sublimest thing we know."*
> *-- David Grayson*

Do not be misled. The loving leader is a tough and thinking leader. Employees like to have leaders who care about their work and who care about them:

> *"A good man likes a hard boss. I don't mean a nagging boss or a grouchy boss. I mean a boss who insists on things being done right and on time; a boss who is watching things closely enough so that he knows a good job from a poor one. Nothing is more discouraging to a good man than a boss who is not on the job, and who does not know whether things are going well or badly."*
> *-- William Feather*

Selah

Take a moment to pause and reflect on this chapter.

Have you viewed leaders, employees, and followers as economic means to an end, as Adam Smith believed? Or, have you looked at leaders, employees, and followers as relationships?

Have you considered love to be a foundational value in the organization?

Record your thoughts about those people with whom you work. What would you like those people to think about you? Do you think the people in your organization demonstrate *agapao* love to you? Why or why not? Do you need to change your belief about people? Where would you like to start?

Chapter 2: The Value of Being Poor in Spirit

This chapter builds on the last chapter and expands into the values that are built on the foundation of *agapao* love. These values comprise the first half of the Sermon on the Mount, a powerful message from Jesus on lifestyle and behavior as recorded in the Gospel according to Matthew. Augustine referred to this sermon as the highest standard of morality and as the perfect measure of the Christian life (Kissinger, 1975, p. 13).

Thomas Aquinas considered the messages from the Sermon on the Mount as wise counsel, and he differentiated these counsels from commandments by describing commandments as obligations, whereas counsels were options left up to each person who heard them (Kissinger, 1975, p. 13). Most commentaries that I have read refer to The Sermon on the Mount as the basis for ethical behavior, which makes it fitting that this is where we continue the discussion of *agapao* as moral or ethical love and how we can apply these values to leadership.

To help set the stage for chapters two through eight it might help to take a brief review of The Beatitudes.

The Beatitudes

The Beatitudes are comprised of the 10 verses from Matthew 5:3-12. These 10 verses contain observable values and one statement of warning. While verses can help us consider Scripture, the use of verses sometimes creates a false sense of separation in the thoughts expressed by the original writers. This is the case in The Beatitudes. While popular translations of the Bible separate The Beatitudes into verses, the original Greek shows them as one continuous flowing thought! Likewise, as leaders, we must take The Beatitudes as a whole concept and not as an a la carte menu.

Each statement of counsel in The Beatitudes begins with the Greek word *makarios*, which translates into English as *"blessed." Makarios* is akin to the Hebrew word *shalom*. Myron Augsburger helps us understand the relationship of *makarios* to *shalom* when he describes the word *makarios* as "incorporating the meaning of wholeness, of joy, of well-being, of holistic peace . . . of the condition of inner satisfaction expressed by Jesus in John 14:27 'My peace I give unto you: not as the world giveth' (KJV)" (Augsburger, 1982, p. 63).

The original Greek leaves out the verb form of "to be" thus removing the sense of time. These words of counsel are timeless, neither to the future, past, nor present, but in all time and throughout all time.

In my studies of the values presented in The Beatitudes, I have come to realize that they exist in Scripture in a sequence. Not only do the rewards expressed in the Scripture increase as the reader works through the statements, but there is also an order of the most common problems from the earlier statements to the later statements. In my consulting work with organizations, I find that the first Beatitude today addresses the most prominent challenge of leadership. The second most prominent challenge that leaders face is addressed by the second Beatitude; and so on down the list. When you read The Beatitudes below, read them as one thought, inseparable, with the view of timeless application.

Matthew 5:3-12   *Humble*

3 Blessed are the poor in spirit, for theirs is the kingdom of heaven.

          Care Deeply

4 Blessed are those who mourn for they will be comforted.

5 Blessed are the meek, for they will inherit the earth.

6 Blessed are those who hunger and thirst for righteousness, for they will be filled.

7 Blessed are the merciful, for they will be shown mercy.

8 Blessed are the pure in heart for they will see God.

9 Blessed are the peacemakers, for they will be called sons of God.

10 Blessed are those who are persecuted because of righteousness, for theirs is the kingdom of heaven.

11 Blessed are you when people insult you, persecute you and falsely say all kinds of evil against you because of me.

12 Rejoice and be glad, because great is your reward in heaven, for in the same way they persecuted the prophets who were before you.

Blessed are the poor in spirit for theirs is the kingdom of heaven.

"Poor in spirit" is a state of being opposite of "rich in pride." What a paradox! Leaders are always looking up to the person who is "king of the hill," the one who is full of bravado and proud of his accomplishments. This Beatitude says to avoid that pride and to see yourself as being empty. Why empty, you wonder? Because an empty cup can hold more and a full cup can receive nothing more. To be poor in spirit is to recognize that you can hold more, and to recognize this means that you must be humble. Some might argue that even a full cup can hold more if you stretch the cup. A potter can enlarge a clay cup by stretching and pulling on the clay. However, this makes the walls thinner and more fragile. I have watched many leaders "thicken their walls" from the inside in order to gain better protection and, in the end, held less in their cup. The opposite of this occurs when leaders willingly show their weakness by admitting that they don't know all that they should.

The Greek words used in this Beatitude translate into "Blessed are you poor," (Baker, 1963, p. 30) which connotes someone who knows that he is poor. This is an excellent definition for one who is humble. Scripture is replete with references of the need to be, and remain, humble. Isaiah 26:5 talks of God humbling those who dwell on high. Matthew 18:4 and 23:12 speak of the need to be humble. Isaiah 66:2 refers to the person who is humble and contrite in spirit. Spirit in the Isaiah passage is the Hebrew word *ruwach* that translates as "the spirit of a rational being." The Greek word used in Matthew 5:3 is *pneuma*, translated as "human spirit" or "rational soul."

I recall visiting with a professor/researcher (name and topical area of expertise withheld to insure confidentiality) who came to my university to speak at a conference in which I was involved. This professor was at the "top of the heap" when it came to his special area of research. I was just beginning my research endeavors and certainly, by comparison to his stature in the field, I was a mere insignificant professor. This great professor (and I use the phrase with true respect) was beginning to look at the life and teaching of Jesus as a source of wisdom on leadership.

During breakfast with him, I was explaining what we were doing at Regent University and how we were using Scripture to teach students about leadership. I was amazed when this man leaned forward and excitedly stated that he was fascinated with what we were doing and asked if I could teach him more about the application of Scripture to leadership. Here, right before me, was an example of being poor in spirit. The *"king of the hill"* in leadership research (actually one of many since the field is so broad with many sub-areas – he was/is the top of one sub-area) was asking me to teach him. I wonder how many of our organizations would do better if the leader leaned across the desk and excitedly asked each employee to teach him or her about what the employee has learned. To be willing to ask for help is first of all, an admonition of the need for help.

Since this first Beatitude counsels the leader to be humble rather than haughty, this ties into the scriptural admonition to not *"lord it over"* the employees (Matthew 20:24-28). The leader who is poor of spirit knows that his employees are intelligent people who, many times, know more of the details of the job and thus, have worthwhile advice to give. This is a key premise of total quality leadership -- to teach the employees how to solve problems, develop solutions, and then trust them to do the work. A humble leader does not lord over his employees or force answers and solutions upon them.

Respect

A humble leader shows respect to all, whether they are superiors or subordinates, because the leader who is poor in spirit recognizes that many people know more than he or she does and, as such, shows respect to everyone. This concept of respect is very important to consider. Would you rather work for someone who treats you with respect or who treats you as dirt to be walked upon? The answer is obvious. We all look forward to working with leaders who are kind, considerate, and who look upon us as co-workers rather than as slaves.

Humbleness

Humbleness of spirit is important for an organization to meet its mission. Humble leaders place the goals of the organization above their own goals. Haughty leaders only look for how the organization can help them to achieve their own goals.

This humbleness does not mean poor in finances or ability. I know a wonderful man who, some time ago, retired from an international bank as senior vice-president (the number two spot in a multinational firm). He was certainly wealthy in terms of cash. He received lavish compensation during his career and invested excess earnings into a sizable fortune. He owned homes in both Seattle and Palm Springs and enjoyed playing golf all over the world. All of this aside, the first characteristic that people attributed to this man was his humility. He listened to those who spoke, and placed the needs of others before his own needs. His employees remained incredibly loyal to him and spent many extra hours accomplishing the work of the organization because they delighted in serving with him rather than being mere tools for him to use and discard.

Similarly, the essence of excellent customer service is the subjugation of our own interest, feelings, and self-aggrandizement to the needs, wants, and desires of our clients. Ken Blanchard, in his book, *Raving Fans*, consistently shows how leaders create *"raving fans"* among customers and employees by placing their own interests behind the interests of their clients and employees.

Sometimes, when you yield to another, you feel like you are losing something. But the paradox of Jesus' teaching is that even when you feel like you are losing, you are still winning. My banking friend was humble and consistently rose to the top. Blanchard's case studies describe people whose companies do well and improve daily. Clients flock to companies that delight them. Employees gravitate to humble leaders who treat them well.

Humbleness does not mean avoiding the limelight. After all, a great actor goes on stage to serve his customers and to delight his audience and he places his entire being into the performance. He feels satisfied if he does his best. If the audience feels satisfied enough to applaud, so much the better. If the audience gives a standing ovation, he accepts it warmly and appreciatively, and the next morning, continues with rehearsal to ensure that he delights the next client. The applause is icing on the cake and is akin to the saying "money follows ministry." If the actor sets out only to gain a standing ovation, he serves himself rather than others, and real, long-term success is doubtful. The paradox is fascinating; instead of trying to achieve, try to serve and delight, and success will follow; try to succeed for selfish gain and failure will follow.

> *"Great men suffer hours of depression through introspection and self-doubt. That is why they are great. That is why you will find modesty and humility the characteristics of such men. "*
> *-- Bruce Barton*

How much more could a humble leader accomplish with eight employees working hard to please him, compared to a haughty leader with eight employees who could care less if the leader lived or died?

Blessed is the leader who is poor in spirit, for his shall be the kingdom of heaven.

Selah

Take a moment to pause and reflect on this chapter.

If I asked your employees the following questions, how would they answer?

Is your leader teachable?

Does your leader seek your opinions and recommendations?

Does your leader demonstrate respect to you in all situations?

Does your leader demonstrate humbleness?

How do people respond when you mention who you work for? Do people indicate that they wish they worked with that leader too? Or, do they give you condolences?

After reflecting on the answers, what can you do to improve your value of being poor in spirit?

Chapter 3: The Value of Caring for Employees/Followers

I used to see The Beatitudes as separate elements or factors of *agapao* leadership. Each value had an equal weight. But as I have taught and consulted with organizations and used The Beatitudes in my consulting with leaders, I have noticed that the first Beatitude, *"poor in spirit,"* seems to surface the most often. The next most frequently occurring Beatitude is the Beatitude that we will look at next, mourning. The other Beatitudes seemed to occur with a relative frequency that matched the sequence of The Beatitudes as they occur in Scripture. How simple it seems that we have the main values stated for us and that The Beatitudes appear in the order of importance as well.

Leaders who are poor in spirit are frequently described as humble, teachable, and show respect for followers. But how does this apply to The Beatitude about mourning? Let's find out.

Blessed are those who mourn for they will be comforted.

Here we receive instruction to mourn because we will be comforted. This is not a popular worldly perspective; in fact, the world seeks out those who are happy and excited. We smile at the jokes of the salesman and gather at the table of the motivational speaker so the speaker can fire us up with enthusiasm. Why then would we want to become mourners?

The Greek word that we translate as *"to mourn,"* is the strongest of the Greek words that implore a deep mourning and longing with the intensity as if mourning for the dead (Augsburger, 1982, p. 63), but since we are focused on the

28

living leader, we can consider this word to show the intensity at which we mourn for those around us. According to Augsburger (1982), to mourn in this fashion is to care deeply. For today's leaders this means to care for the organization, the clients that we serve, our employees, our superiors, and even to care for the condition of our competitors. This is not an exhaustive list, but rather a beginning. Augsburger added that to mourn this deeply is to draw closer to God and for God to draw closer to you (p. 63).

The Greek word that we translate as *"mourn"* is *penteo*, which is the act or feeling of mourning or bewailing. This is an active tense verb that implies a continuation of action. Think of the leader who cares so much about his employees, his clients, his company, his market, his superiors, and his competitors that he literally is in mourning for their condition. This state of mourning also includes the characterization of deep concern. It does not imply that the leader goes around the office crying, yelling, beating his chest, and pulling out his hair. It does imply that there is great concern for others.

Have you ever worked for someone who cared about you, who really cared? Loyalty and devotion to task and company grow out of trust and the knowledge of protection that comes from the employment relationship. Employees who know that the leader has their interests at heart are willing to commit themselves to corporate tasks. This is the same condition that Scripture says must exist between husband and wife. The husband must care so much for his wife that he filters every decision through the question *"is it in the best interest of my wife?"*

Consider what it would be like to work for a leader who was so concerned about you that he treated you as a co-worker, (from the first Beatitude) and cared so deeply about you that he made decisions with your best interests in mind. This is certainly not the typical United States leader.

The paradox of Jesus' teaching is that whoever is to be first, must be last, or at least should consider himself last. Great leaders do not seek to be number one; they become number one because their employees make them number one. Innovation in a company is always at the discretion of the employees. As they say, you can lead a horse to water, but you can't make it drink. In this same way, you can lead an employee to the edge of innovation and excellence, but you cannot make him or her jump the line to improvement. People will only innovate because they want to. William Arnold's book, *The Human Touch*, gives us an inside look at a CEO who cared for and mourned for his employees. The employees of the Hospital Corporation of America, from the vice-president of finance to the janitors and the valet parking attendants, consistently sought ways to improve the organization. In spite of being a good leader, Arnold still had to address the problem of some employees not believing that he cared. So he learned to do this in an unusual way. He removed his office door and had it mounted on a stand in the main entrance to the building with a sign that indicated that his office was always open. To prove it, here was the door!! In time, the employees came to know that Arnold cared about his people, and he always stopped and visited with employees as he walked about the building.

I struggled with this Beatitude during my journey of trying to develop more of these values and to become an *agapao* leader. If I made sure that an employee received his or her paycheck and the check cleared the bank -- what more did I need to do? I was amazed at the transformation in my

30

thinking that occurred during the first three years after making a commitment to my employees to become an *agapao* leader. In particular, I recall one spring day when I arrived at work and it dawned on me that the local public schools would be closing for summer break in three weeks. Normally I would have dismissed this as unnecessary trivia, but in my mind I thought about the employees who worked with me. Four of the employees had children in public schools and either both parents worked or the employee was the single head of household. I went to each of the four employees who had children in school and who fit the criteria of both parents working or single head of household and asked if there was anything that I or the organization could do to improve the employees' soon-to-be increased responsibility of having children at home for the summer. Each employee appeared a bit surprised that I brought up the issue. Each employee asked to have a day to think about it before answering.

The next day, each of the four employees spent a few minutes discussing with me their upcoming changes in family settings. The first employee indicated that her husband began working in the early morning and would arrive home at around 2 p.m. each day. If she could delay starting her workday until 10 a.m. and then work later in the evening, she would have no problem finding day care with neighbors for four hours until her husband came home.

The second employee indicated that her mother was arriving for the summer and would help with the childcare. This employee, though, asked if she could take a longer lunch break to visit with her mother and children. She offered, like the first employee, to work later hours to insure that all the work was completed.

The third employee did not have the benefit of in-house assistance, but felt that her children were old enough to take care of themselves for a few hours a day. She asked if she could work six days a week for six hours a day. This, she thought would allow her to handle the increased childcare responsibility.

The fourth employee came to me and indicated that her daughter was now old enough to take care of herself and that childcare was no longer a concern. However, the employee had worked throughout her daughter's life and the employee wanted desperately to spend some time with her daughter. This employee asked if she could work four, ten-hour days and take Fridays off to spend with her daughter. Since her husband worked on Friday, this would give her time to spend alone with her daughter. In each of the four cases, there was no specific requirement for the employees to be in the office at a set time. We did not have a receptionist position, so no one had to be in a set place at a set time.

In looking at each of the requests, there was no reason that we could not accommodate the employees, so I agreed to the various work schedules. I have to admit that I was a bit concerned and envisioned a summer of mayhem and anarchy in the office. But this time, the professor learned the lesson. The office ran smoothly and we actually got more work done that summer than any other similar period. Later, I heard from employees, that since I cared enough about them to adjust the work schedules, they felt more committed to the organization, which resulted in higher productivity.

You may be wondering what would happen when an employee has to be in the office at a set time, like a receptionist. This situation occurred a year or so later. In this situation, the receptionist received assistance from other employees who helped cover the receptionist's duties when she could not be at the desk. And like the other times, it was a productive summer with vast amounts of work being completed on schedule.

Let me share another story of a person who lived out this Beatitude and cared for his employees. One of his employees was faced with a difficult maternity situation and, while the child was fine at birth, the employee was not left in good health. She was strong enough to leave the hospital and to go home to her husband and other two children, but the employee had used all of her available sick leave and vacation and was now on disability pay, which provided about 80 percent of what the employee made prior to taking maternity leave. The husband had recently lost his job and spent all day every day looking for work.

The leader heard from one of the other employees in the organization that this employee was not recovering very well, that the family had run out of money, and that their refrigerator was out of food. The leader explained the problem to his wife and his wife asked if she could help. The leader and his wife bought $100 worth of groceries and the wife delivered them to the employee. This helped lift the spirits of the employee. What was the end result? If you guessed that the employee's loyalty and work ethic improved -- you're right. The paradox continues -- seek what is right and care for your employees and they will care for you.

A leader living by spiritual principles might organize an effort to collect sick leave from employees and give it to an employee who is on long-term disability. I remember doing just that in a company that I owned in Alaska. One of our office employees suffered a devastating trailer fire. She lost all of her possessions and received second and third degree

33

burns over most of her body. Although we had an excellent medical plan and long-term disability insurance, the long-term disability still did not pay 100 percent of her salary. I granted her two months of paid leave and then I asked all of the employees to donate any vacation time that they could spare so that the burned employee could stay on full salary as long as possible.

The company had both union and non-union workers. The union shop steward and I worked well together and usually we resolved issues quietly and quickly. The steward informed me that some of the employees were reluctant to give vacation hours since the burned employee earned less per hour than union wages and because the employees felt that the company would gain in the transfer. I assured the steward that my interest was with the burned employee and that the idea of an <u>in</u>equitable exchange rate did not enter into the transaction. I realized that no one knew I had given the employee two months of paid leave. I told the steward of what I had already done on behalf of the employee and offered to convert all hours from the donors to the burned employee on a dollar-to-dollar basis. Thus, if a union employee earned one and one-half times what the burned employee earned, then each hour from the union employee would convert to one and one-half hours for the burned employee. The union employees gave the burned employee a total of four months of vacation time! This allowed the employee to recuperate without fear of additional economic loss. There are many ways to demonstrate sacrificial love for employees.

Caring About Payroll

Before I began my journey to become an *agapao* leader, I didn't concern myself with what our employees earned in salary and hourly rates. The university's human resource department determined the rates and scales and there wasn't anything most of us could do about it -- or so I thought. One day, I noticed that a couple of the employees who worked with me were looking rather tired and worn out. After some conversation, it became clear that the employees were working other jobs in an effort to earn enough money to pay the bills and to keep the collectors away from the doors. I looked at the amount of money that we provided in payroll and worked out a minimum budget for a single person to live comfortably (not lavishly and not in poverty) here in the local area. After determining the net and the gross salary, it was clear that we were not paying these two employees enough to live on by themselves, much less to raise a child on.

To test my concept of what I called a "minimum living wage," I asked my MBA students who were taking my class in people leadership, to form groups of three students and to do the same exercise I did -- calculate the minimum salary, before taxes, for a single person living in the vicinity of the university. The students' answers were similar to those that I calculated. At that time, the minimum wage was just below $5.00 an hour and all of the students determined that the minimum living wage was $10.50 an hour.

When I saw the answers, I was sure that the obvious brilliance of the connection between values and behavior (paying people a minimum wage) would be clear in the students' minds. After the exercise, I asked the students to tell me what minimum wage they would offer a person in the future. I was taken back a bit when most of the students answered $5.00. When I asked, "Why so low?" the students responded that it was a government minimum and there was nothing they could do. I was surprised to see how easily we can slip back into non-*agapao* thinking. I decided then and there that I would do all I could to raise the income of my employees to at least the minimum living wage. I was able to raise the salaries of the two employees that I mentioned earlier. When their salaries went up, they both quit their second jobs and they experienced a sense of peace –in their households (more on peace later in The Beatitudes). Since that time, I have won some of the efforts to raise employees' salaries to the minimum living wage and I have lost in other efforts. I am committed, though, to continuing the efforts to raise salaries wherever I can.

This concept of the minimum living wage can be found in Matthew 20:1-16 in the parable of the vineyard in which the owner pays the workers who worked half a day the same wages as those who worked all day. The amount of payment was a denarius that represented the amount of money that it took for a day's living – food, shelter, etc. So, the owner made sure that everyone had enough to live on. Now, I know the parables are all for spiritual lessons but isn't it interesting how Jesus used everyday settings to build a parable? How are you doing with your minimum living wage? Do you know how much it takes for someone to live?

Blessed are those leaders who mourn for their employees and their customers, for they will be comforted and see improvement.

Caring About Rest

We live in a hard-charging, high-involvement world. Phrases like 24/7/365 are common. For those of you who are fortunate enough not to know what this phrase means, it means that service is provided 24 hours a day, 7 days a week, 365 days a year. No rest! For most of us, the Sabbath is a day to get all of the laundry done, buy all of the groceries, or do all of the yard work.

I grew up in a rural farming community in Nebraska and understood what it meant to let ground go fallow. Farmers generally prefer to plant crops every season in order to gain as much as possible from the soil, but they also know that allowing the ground to rest produces more crops in the future. While we can do a lot with chemicals to replenish the nutrients in the ground, there is nothing like rest. *Agapao* leaders understand that their employees need rest and the leaders do what is necessary to insure that employees get the rest that they need.

As my experience with *agapao* leadership developed, I had a new problem to deal with at work, people wanted to be in the office! What a problem to have. At first, I was excited that everyone was always at work, until I realized that by staying at work longer than the normal work day, I was unintentionally allowing employees to not interact with their families and to not get the rest that they needed. I found myself trying to get employees to leave. I would stop by on Saturday or Sunday to get something that I had left in the office and I would find people working. Each time when I asked the person why he or she was in the office the answer was that he or she thought of something that needed to be done and wanted to take care of it. My hardest problem was keeping people out of the office!

I have pondered this idea of organizational rest and have concluded thus far, that our organizational leaders don't know much about it. We talk about sabbaticals at the university, but the professor who goes on a sabbatical has to work just as hard as usual, only on something different than

37

the usual teaching and research. This is more in line with the concept of crop rotation than the concept of letting ground go fallow.

What does it mean to give an employee rest? It doesn't mean vacation, since most of us in the United States expend more energy on vacation than we do at work -- what about a real rest? What about allowing the employee to go "fallow" every seventh year? What would it be like? When I mentioned this at a seminar, one of the people in attendance commented that we couldn't take the increase in payroll costs. The seminar attendee commented that payroll would go up by a full $1/7^{th}$ perhaps, or perhaps not. If people are more rested, the productivity might be higher. In my theory, I noted that the productivity levels went up so much that total payroll costs went down. Many of our employees were spouses of students, and when the student graduated, it was natural for the graduate to look for work and for the family to move. When an employee left, the remaining employees would offer to divide up the work or re-organize the work. A by-product of all of the increased productivity was that employees had free time. An interesting book entitled, *The Myth of Measurement*, examines what happened to the economy every time the federal minimum wage increased. In each case, there was a small decline in the economy followed by an increase in the economy that more than compensated for the initial downturn. I have to wonder; if we follow God's principles of rest, shouldn't we see an increase in total output? God's principles are really quite simple in cause and effect.

Organizational Selah

In addition to the pause and reflect section at the end of each chapter in this book, I wanted to raise the concept of

Organizational *Selah*. After a major project or event in your organization do you take time with the employees to pause and reflect? We started doing this in the organization with which I am currently employed. After a major project, the employees meet for a half-day to just pause and reflect on the project. During this time we consider what went well and what did not go well. We reflect on the project and how it tied to our organizational purpose and mission. We use a tape recorder to capture the thoughts and then transcribe the comments at a later date. We plan the *Selah* meeting so that food is available and that the meeting is intentionally informal and slow paced. The meeting usually lasts a half-day, and all employees can then go home to rest if they wish. We have found the results of these *Selah* experiences invaluable to all of us.

Let's review what it might be like to work for a leader who has the first two Beatitudes as foundational values. The leader would be teachable, as well as willingly and openly admitting that he or she doesn't know as much as others about a topic. The leader would care so deeply about his or her followers that every decision would be made with the employees' best interests in mind. Who wouldn't want to work for someone like this? With just the first two Beatitudes we have an excellent leader.

Selah

If I asked your employees whether you, as a leader, care for them, what would I hear from them?

How are you doing at paying, at least the minimum living wage? Do you know what your local minimum living wage is? If not, now is a good time to get some of your HR people working to determine what it takes for a single adult to live (not lavish or in poverty) in your local area.

How are you doing at getting the right rest? What about your employees?

When you talk to employees about having a retreat, what do they think? Will it be lots of work in a different location? Will there be a chance to pause and reflect? If not the latter, you might want to try taking a break.

Do you take time to pause and reflect after a major project?

Do you really know the condition of your employees? Do you really care? Can you imagine that God's principles, when actively employed by you and others, can benefit your organization?

Chapter 4: The Value of Controlled Discipline

The third Beatitude is about discipline and is related to the second Beatitude about caring for employees. As we examine the third Beatitude try to see how caring is a related value.

Blessed are the meek for they will inherit the earth.

Today's typical leader abhors the word meek since leaders want employees to know that they are the Boss, which is supported in the popular leadership press with books on tough negotiation styles and in business magazine articles about the toughest bosses in the toughest companies. Amazingly, though, true to form, Jesus' counsel shows the depth of the paradox of *agapao* leadership and in the characteristics that He seeks to develop in us.

The Greek word for meek is *praus*, or humility, which continues the theme of humility from the first Beatitude. Though this is not a repetition of the first Beatitude, it is an application of humility to behavior, since you can also find *praus* in conjunction with action. The Greek term is a rich term and more fully is translated into "controlled discipline." In line with this application of meekness to behavior, Aristotle spoke of meekness as the means between anger and indifference (Augsburger, 1982, p. 63). Aristotle described one who is meek as being angry on the right occasion with the right people at the right moment and for the right length of time (Boice, 1972, p. 37). Thus, we might see that the meek have a sense of duty and that they demonstrate controlled discipline.

41

John Wesley in his Sermon 22 entitled *"Upon our Lord's Sermon on the Mount – Discourse 2"* provides some insight into the concept of meek. Wesley said:

> "[t]he meek are zealous for the Lord of hosts; but their zeal is always guided by knowledge, and tempered, in every thought, and word, and work, with the love of man, as well as the love of God. They do not desire to extinguish any of the passions, which God has for wise ends implanted in their nature; but they have the master of all. They hold them all in subjection, and employ them only in subservience to those ends. And thus even the harsher and more unpleasing passions are applicable to the noblest purposes. "

Barclay stated that selfish anger is always a sin but selfless anger can be one of the great moral dynamics of the world (Barclay, 1958, p. 91). We see this controlled selfless anger in Jesus as He swept the moneychangers out of the temple. The psalmist wrote of the meek inheriting the earth (Psalm 37:11). The Hebrew word used by the psalmist here is *anayv* that translates as gentle in mind or circumstances. It also connotes saintliness. Let us examine Jesus' behaviors in the temple as recorded in Matthew 1:12-13; Mark 11:15-17; Luke 19:45-46; and John 2:12-16 – the greatest detail comes from the account in the Gospel of John, so this analysis relies more on the passage in John. Jesus saw that people were using a part of the temple in a manner that defiled its sanctity. The temple courts were not to be used for commerce of any kind. Commerce could and did occur at the temple, but commerce was meant to be restricted to outside of the temple.

John recorded that Jesus made a whip out of cords (v. 15) and drove the cattle and sheep from the temple. Here, the Messiah, the one who could turn water into wine, make fig trees wither, heal the sick, and raise the dead, took the time to make a whip out of cords and to move the cattle and sheep out of the building. Why? The cattle and sheep were not at fault. Can you imagine what most of us would have done if we had possessed the same power as Jesus? I think, in my own uncontrolled anger, I would have turned the cattle into a few thousand fast-food hamburgers and made a spectacle large enough to keep the crowds talking for days!

Verse 15 goes on to say that he scattered the coins. I doubt that I would have been so controlled. If I had the power that Jesus possessed, I think, that in my uncontrolled anger, I would have melted the coins into the stone floor so that the coins spelled out *"Jesus was here!"* Talk about leaving a sign! But then, if I had done this, the coins would not have been of any use to anyone and would have been as wasted as the thousands of fast-food hamburgers I would have made. And what about the doves that John wrote of in verse 16? Jesus demanded that the people remove the birds. Why didn't Jesus scatter the cages? Or, at least open the cages and let the doves fly. Why not just let them go? Because the doves would have been lost and the people would have suffered. Jesus was not interested in hurting anyone; He wanted the temple restored to its intended use.

Would I have been so controlled as to ask someone to remove the doves? I don't think I would have. I think I might have done something less controlled. And what would have been the result of my actions? Put yourself in the place of the people conducting commercial business, and Jesus has just destroyed your property and removed part of your livelihood. Would you be willing to listen to the message of Christ after that? Most folks, I think, would not listen to a leader who had reacted in such uncontrolled ways.

This is the essence of controlled discipline; it draws people closer to you, whereas uncontrolled discipline drives people away. Leadership occurs only at the point of contact between leader and follower, and if this contact is broken or prevented through uncontrolled discipline for example, leadership won't occur. The follower may comply with the leader's commands, but the follower will not commit. Compliance and capitulation, are not leadership – they are coercion.

Let's look at another biblical example of a meek man, Moses. "Now the man Moses was very meek, above all the men who were upon the face of the earth" (Numbers 12:3). Note that this passage describes Moses as being above all the men who were upon the face of the earth. Not your idea of a mild-mannered little man with limited strength and force-of-will. Moses defeated the gods of Egypt, conquered Pharaoh, led a million people out of bondage, fed and cared for them for over 40 years, laid down the Mosaic Law, and established the foundation for the promised land of Israel. All in all, this is a wonderful example of leadership, but Moses did not do this alone, for God worked through him to accomplish all these feats. God can only work through the humbleness, the mourning, and the disciplined anger of those leaders who, as empty vessels, are filled by Him.

Baker uses Charles Wesley's hymn to demonstrate the strength of controlled discipline:

> Jesus' tremendous name
> Puts all our foes to flight:

> Jesus, the meek, the angry Lamb
> A Lion is in fight.
> By all hell's host withstood,
> We all hell's host o 'erthrow:
> And conquering them, through Jesus' blood,
> We still to conquer go. (Baker, 1963, p. 44)

Baker continues his definition of meek by saying, "the meek man never submits to evil or compromises with it, but by active, persistent patience overcomes it" (Baker, 1963, p. 45). Bauman gives us another view of meek in his description of one who is meek as being a wild animal that, upon domestication, is still just as capable of feats of strength, yet is gentle with people. Bauman repeats his definition as "power under control" (Bauman, 1981, p. 56).

First Hand Experience with the Controlled Discipline that Bauman Describes

I recall a time back in my youth; it seems like a very long time ago now as I think back to the early 1960s, when I encountered just such an animal as Bauman describes. My grandmother owned a piece of land in the Sand Hills of Nebraska and decided to sell the parcel of land to her cousin who wanted the land to add to his ranch. Since my grandmother wanted the cash for retirement, it seemed like a good deal for both, and to celebrate the transaction, my grandmother and my mother decided that the three of us would go from our little town near Omaha, Nebraska, and spend a long weekend with the relatives out in the Sand Hills which is in the upper western area of the state. The land consists of rolling hills of sand (hence the name) with sparse grass and minimally planted ground. It takes a lot of land to raise cattle because of the sparse grass. In some places there are meadows that support small hay-growing fields.

I had worked on farms around our little town and looked forward to seeing how a ranch differed from a farm. The three of us drove to the ranch and spent the evening visiting with relatives. My grandmother's cousin asked if I wanted to go with the men in the morning and work in the hay field. I eagerly agreed to get out of the house to engage in some physical activity, and since I had worked on several farms bailing hay and moving it to the barns, I thought I might be able to help.

The next morning, my grandmother's cousin woke me up at 5 a.m., a bit early for haying work I thought, but *"when on the ranch you do as the ranch hands do."* So I quickly dressed and joined the men in the kitchen for a cup of coffee and some breakfast. I didn't like coffee, but as a young lad, I wanted to be part of the group. After a quick breakfast, we all headed out the door. I expected to find a pick-up truck that would take us out to the hay field or a tractor and flatbed cart used to haul hay from the field to the barns. I was a bit surprised when I was handed the reins to a horse -- a big horse.

I had ridden a horse a few times, so I was not completely naïve, but I was certainly not a skilled rider. The big mare that I was assigned to was, according to grandmother's cousin, a gentle mare that would be fine to ride. Here it was, still dark and cold in the morning, I drank coffee I didn't like, and then I was stuck with this horse. My attitude was not the most pleasant, I admit.

I managed to get into the saddle, although it was not a picture of grace and skill. I recalled from my brief training in horsemanship at the Boy Scout Camp the previous summer, that I should hold the reins firmly, but not to cause the horse discomfort from the bit, and let the animal know that I was in

46

command of the situation. The rest of the men started out, and I kicked this big mare in the ribs to get her going. The mare, upon being kicked, turned her head and looked at me with a look that was of pure disgust and disdain! The mare snorted a bit and turned her head back to watch the other horses and riders head down the dirt roadway. Thinking that all I needed to do was to establish authority I once again kicked the big mare in the sides and gave the old cowboy shout: "*Giddy-up.*" The mare turned and looked at me with contempt in her eyes and tried to bite my left leg. I quickly remembered that this was an animal that could throw me off her back and trounce me into the dirt if she really wanted to. But fortunately for me, she had decided not to do so and was allowing me to get my self-directed efforts for control out of my system. It was clear that the horse was the stronger of the two of us and that she had controlled her discipline, thus sparing me a trouncing that I probably deserved.

As I relaxed my hold on the reins I quietly told the mare that I was sorry and that she could do what she wanted, the mare nodded her head, snorted, and started off down the road toward the other horses. I don't think she understood my words, but she must have understood the change in my attitude or position in the saddle, since communication obviously happened. Her gait was a bit fast and uncomfortable, but we soon caught up with the rest of the riders and she settled down into a relaxed pace.

As I read Bauman's statement, the image of that big mare returned to my memory, and I understood the focus of this third Beatitude. I had learned an important lesson that day, but I have to admit that the lesson didn't sink in until I read Bauman's statement years later.

Leaders Seek to Understand the Situation before Administering Discipline

Here's another example that may help you understand controlled discipline. I can't go into all of the details since it would violate the confidentiality of the people involved, so I will summarize. The situation involved an employee who we hired for her administrative skills, attention to detail, and her follow-through in getting projects done. I assigned her to help me with three key projects that were very important to me.

Everything seemed to go well in the beginning and the employee seemed to have a good grasp of the concepts and the needs. However, the first report after a couple of weeks indicated that the employee had mixed up the three projects. After I had a couple of meetings with the employee, it seemed that the employee had it all straight and we headed down the path again. Two weeks later, though, the problems resurfaced. Key guests were not invited to the events and unwanted guests were invited. By this time, it appeared doubtful to me that the employee was capable of doing the work and that I was looking at the potential failure of the three.

My first reaction was to call the employee into my office and to terminate her, at least from this area of responsibility, and to consider reassigning her. However, I decided that if I were really serious about wanting to lead according to The Beatitudes, then I would have to control the discipline and see what might be going on behind the scenes. Surprisingly, the employee called me and asked to talk with me about her performance. When the employee entered my office, it was clear that something was not right. The employee apologized for poor performance and explained that for the past three months the employee's home life had been, and continued to be, in turmoil. The employee's spouse was talking about leaving the family and tempers at home were high. Their two children were becoming problematic as a reaction to all the trouble between the parents.

I realized during the conversation that this Beatitude on controlled discipline was directly tied to the Beatitude about mourning. Had I been more attuned to this employee's demeanor and behavior in the office, I might have recognized the characteristics of deeper problems and I would have intervened earlier and discussed workloads and assignments. While I may not have been able to help the home situation, I could have restructured assignments, thus, reducing the added burden of working on a high-profile assignment. The risk of failure on the project only added to the problems that the employee faced. Here, I had contributed to the problem and, had I acted outside of The Beatitudes, I might have fired the employee for incompetence all the time feeling that I was a good leader for not tolerating her poor performance.

The poor performance in this situation was my own poor leadership of not being aware of the condition of my flock. At least, by exercising controlled discipline and seeking to understand, I prevented myself from making a terrible leadership mistake and from making this employee's life worse. We did shift duties, and eventually the problems worked out to the good of all those involved.

How Do Leaders Control Discipline?

So how will you exhibit controlled discipline as a leader? Are you like Jesus in the temple chasing out cattle and sheep, or like Moses leading the Hebrews out of Egypt, or, are you like Bruce Winston riding a big horse across the Nebraska Sand Hills?

First, understand that as a leader you have power, power to reward, to punish, to promote, to ignore, to provide resources, or not to provide resources. Followers know this and fear their leaders out of concern for what happens when leaders engage in uncontrolled discipline.

Discipline is for correction and reproof, not for punishment. Discipline begins with patience as depicted in Proverbs 14:29 (NIV): "A patient man has great understanding but a quick-tempered man displays folly." This proverb helps us see that understanding results from patience, and it is this understanding that helps the leader know what discipline to give. In most of the situations I encountered along my journey to become an *agapao* leader, I have found that the most often-needed form of discipline is instruction. Usually, problems occur because of a lack of knowledge or skill on the part of the follower. The next most common form of discipline that I have found is a reduction in workload to allow the employee to work through some problem outside of the job. The problem may include personal health issues or family emotional issues. Few of us can perform at peak levels when we are physically ill or wrestling with family problems. Punishing an employee because he or she is physically ill won't do much to improve the long-term performance of the employee.

In another instance, I once had an employee who wasn't producing at the desired level. I talked with the employee and found out that the employee wasn't feeling well and could not maintain a full day's work for more than two days. I asked what the doctors said and the employee informed me that she had not seen a doctor and believed that the matter

Amazon   ISBN : 0972581901

Write an online review.

was a spiritual matter that she had to accept. My discipline
for her was to require her to see a doctor and to continue to
see doctors until all physical reasons for her problems had
been removed.

I am certainly not opposed to the need to work through a
spiritual matter, but I wanted to make sure that all physical
causes of the problem had been removed. Several weeks
later the employee had surgery to fix the physical problem,
and after her recovery she returned to full workloads. I agree
that this is not the typical MBA-textbook example of
discipline, but then I don't think most MBA programs teach
agapao leadership!

There are times when the employee plays a greater role in
the problem. In addition, poor performance can come from
being in the wrong work situation or in a situation of
incorrect levels of supervision.

The situational leadership model developed by Hersey and
Blanchard (1982), tells us that, based on two levels (high and
low), of (1) a person's knowledge of a task and (2)
willingness to perform the task, there are four leadership
styles that can be used – one for each of the four conditions.
If you have an employee who is in a situation that doesn't fit
your leadership style, then the discipline is either for you to
change your style, or for you to help the employee get into a
different situation.

W. E. Deming, who was instrumental in helping the
Japanese become a world-class manufacturing country,
referenced the 85-15 principle. This principle says that 85
percent of employee problems are caused by the system,
which is the responsibility of the leadership. Employees

cause the other 15 percent of the problems. But what about the employee who doesn't seem to care at all?

If the employee doesn't care because he or she is in the wrong job, then the leader has the responsibility to help the employee to find a new job. If the employee just doesn't care, or if rebellion is at the base of the problem, and no system-related cause can be found, then the employee should be removed from the workplace, but removed in such a manner that there is dignity for the employee and sufficient financial support to find a new position. This *"severance"* support varies depending on the employee's job position, the current job market and geographical location. The focus of the severance package is to help and encourage the employee to get started somewhere else.

The Leader with Control

Consider the leader who possesses controlled discipline. He or she never flies off the handle, yells, or shouts. This leader always remains in control of his or her faculties, holds to, and never compromises, those values in order to get the next promotion or to get the client's next big order. People see this leader as a rock of strength and controlled energy, unflappable in the midst of confusion and frustration. The meek leader is someone in whom employees can confide because he or she never strikes back even when others are critical.

Imagine working for a leader like this. Would you give your all for this leader? Would you go the extra mile without being asked? Most employees would.

Blessed are the meek leaders, for their controlled discipline will result in inheriting the earth.

Selah

Take a few minutes to think about a time when a leader for whom you worked, demonstrated controlled discipline. What was your reaction to the leader before and after the situation?

Has there been a time when you reacted and disciplined in an uncontrolled manner? In your opinion, what was the result?

If you have followers who are willing to openly talk to you, ask them to point out past instances of uncontrolled and controlled discipline and have them explain to you how your behavior affected all the followers.

Be brave. It won't be the easiest thing that you have ever done, but it will be one of the best things that you've ever done as a leader!

Chapter 5: The Value of Always Seeking What Is Right

Blessed are those who hunger and thirst for righteousness, for they will be filled.

This Beatitude speaks to the need of the leader to be in a right relationship with: (a) God, (b) with the people around him, and (c) even with himself. It is important to see the intensity with which this Beatitude calls us. The words hunger and thirst in the Greek are *peinao* and *dipsao* meaning, respectively, "famished or crave for," and "to thirst." These words infer an ongoing condition similar to the condition described in Psalm 42:1, 2a: "As the deer pants for streams of water, so my soul pants for you, O God. My soul thirsts for God, for the living God" (NIV). This root word *dikaios* and its derivative *dikaisoune* translate into "holy, just, right(eous), and equity" (of character or act). Thus, we begin to see the unfolding of an ethical leader from this Beatitude. Eric Baker described the person in this way: "the man who is blessed in this respect is the man who above all desires to fulfill the intention of his being and become what he ought to be" (Baker, 1963, p. 55).

This is not the only verse in the Bible that calls us to seek and to do what is good. Two proverbs help us further understand this concept. Proverbs 11:27, "He who seeks good finds goodwill, but evil comes to him who searches for it" (NIV). Proverbs 21:3 instructs us, "To do what is right and just is more acceptable to the Lord than sacrifice" (NIV).

Many presume that this Beatitude means, "seeking after God only." Jesus placed this Beatitude in the fourth position which allows us to see a pattern of asking people: (a) to be

54

humble, (b) to be mournful of the problems and conditions around us, (c) to be controlled in our actions, and (d) to continually seek what is good, what is just, what is right, and what is equitable. Imagine the leader who holds these four characteristics; how wonderful it would be to work with, and for, someone like this.

This Beatitude is in contrast to Adam Smith's foundational belief that the butcher, the brewer, or the baker only do what they do because of what each gains from the transaction. In contrast to Smith, this Beatitude says that the righteous leader does what he or she does because it is the right thing to do. This is a heart issue in that a leader may seek out a long-term relationship with another organization because it is good for both and not because it is good just for the leader's organization.

Here is an example. Recently, I had the opportunity to witness this type of righteous leadership value in action. A department head (let's call him Bob) supported the notion of a new operation in the organization because the new operation would help all of the organization's customers. Budget restrictions, fiscal year start-stop cycles, and bureaucratic red tape prevented the new operation from starting. Bob went to visit Pete, the newly named head of the new operation (or at least Pete would be the new head whenever the new operation would start), and offered to "loan" an employee named Mary, to the new operation. In addition, Bob agreed to pay the payroll expenses for Mary for the next three months until the budget cycles and fiscal year start-stop cycles allowed Pete to begin on his own.

By having Mary work for Pete (and by the way, Mary thought this was a good idea, too) for three months, Pete was able to start the new operation early. Customer responses to

Pete's new operation were overwhelmingly positive and the whole organization improved. Bob's actions were beyond his transactional benefit as Adam Smith might claim. But what about the secondary benefit to Bob's customers from which Bob also benefited? Yes, there were secondary benefits, but Bob received disproportionately less benefit than had Bob simply started his own customer service operation with Mary doing the work. Why then did Bob act this way? Because Bob knew the value to the whole organization, and Bob sought what was right and just.

We have only traveled through the first half of The Beatitudes and already they outline a leader who has more interest in people, who demonstrates more concern, and who has more righteousness than 90 percent of the typical leaders in U.S. organizations today (in my estimation). Jesus builds a perfect leader by starting with a key foundational stone of *agapao* love and then adds character blocks. Each block appears intriguing by itself, but combined with the others, it creates a wonderful building that provides shelter and support for the employees working beneath its roof.

Deciding What to Hunger and Thirst For

Each of us has desires that we hunger and thirst after. Jesus used these verbs for a reason since hunger and thirst are primary needs that are instinctual. Yet, we also hunger and thirst after the unrighteous, the unjust, the inequitable, and the unholy. Jesus recognizes the free will of man and differentiates the leader who seeks what is good from the one who seeks what is not good. Blessed is he who seeks what is good. There is an unstated thought that the one who seeks what is not good will not be blessed – this is confirmed by Proverbs 11:27 mentioned earlier. Notice that there is not a condemnation in this Beatitude, only a support for right behaviors.

Consider what it might be like to work for a leader who always seeks what is right, just, equitable, and holy. The leader constantly looks for opportunities to do good deeds for the organization. The leader constantly tries to ensure that his mind is free of unhealthy thoughts. This leader certainly would not be one whom we would expect to see before a grand jury for embezzlement. This leader could run for national political office with a clear conscience and not even the most *"dogged"* reporter could turn up dirt to shame the leader's character.

I am not describing a holier-than-thou, self-righteous, Bible-thumping, workplace judge of what everyone else should do. Remember the first three Beatitudes. The perfect leader is first, humble. That means that while the leader is seeking righteousness, he does so because he knows it is right. It may not even be a conscious effort; it's just the *"right"* thing. This is the leader whom others talk about with quiet respect and admiration wishing that they could be as good and wondering how the leader does it. It is interesting to point out that if others wish to learn how to be like this perfect leader, they could learn by reading a single text -- the Bible!

How Will You Know the Righteous Leader?

You will know the righteous leader by the evidence of the presence of the Holy Spirit. Isaiah 11:1-5 provides a description of the presence of the Holy Spirit. This passage describes the coming Messiah. The righteous leader will also manifest these same characteristics.

> *A shoot will come up from the stump of Jesse; from his roots a Branch will bear fruit.*

57

> *The Spirit of the LORD will rest on him -- the Spirit of wisdom and of understanding, the Spirit of counsel and of power, the Spirit of knowledge and of the fear of the LORD - and he will delight in the fear of the LORD. He will not judge by what he sees with his eyes, or decide by what he hears with his ears; but with righteousness he will judge the needy, with justice he will give decisions for the poor of the earth.*
>
> *He will strike the earth with the rod of his mouth; with the breath of his lips he will slay the wicked. Righteousness will be his belt and faithfulness the sash around his waist.*

The leader who seeks righteousness will be filled with it. The presence of righteousness is obvious because of the mutual presence of the Spirit of wisdom and understanding, of counsel, and of power, as well as having knowledge of and fear of God. Wisdom and understanding go together.

The Hebrew word for wisdom in the passage above from Isaiah is *chokmah* that is derived from the root *chakam* meaning "to be wise in mind, act, and word; to deal wisely, to make wiser." The action tense "to make" is the key here. The leader's actions tell us whether wisdom is present. The Hebrew word that we translate as "understanding" is *biynah* that derives from *biyn*, which freely translates "to separate mentally." It also translates as "perceive, to be prudent, to teach, think, or cause to make happen." Wisdom means knowing what is right for the situation, and understanding means the ability to put action to the thoughts. Hence, the righteous leader not only knows what is correct, but also implements a plan to cause correct action.

This passage places "counsel" and "power" together to build on each other and to grow from the foundation of wisdom and understanding. *Etsah*, the Hebrew word for counsel, means advice or prudence. It is a word that closely aligns with *yaats*, meaning "to give and take advice, to determine, to purpose, and to guide." The King James Version translates power as "might." Both power and might translate from the Hebrew *gebuwrah* that means "valor, victory, force, mastery, power, strength, and might." This word picture shows us the righteous leader as one who not only knows what is right and devises action steps to bring about correct action, but who also seeks advice and advises people around him or her as to what to do. In addition, he or she possesses the power, strength, or resources to enact the right action.

The Hebrew word for knowledge implies knowledge of Jehovah. The righteous leader knows God and fears Him. This fear is not a fear of cowering and concern for life and limb. Instead, this fear is of respect and acceptance that God is awesome. Have you ever worked for a leader who was so good, so powerful, so knowledgeable, and so capable that you could not help being in awe and amazement? Those who have worked with righteous leaders tell me they are in fear of the greatness of the person, yet the leader does nothing to cause them to be afraid (as in a fear for safety).

This completion of the word picture lets us see that the righteous leader does all things in the knowledge of God and with a deep respect for the person of God manifested as the Holy Spirit.

> *"Fear [the fear of man -- not respect] is an acid which is pumped into one's atmosphere. It causes mental, moral and spiritual asphyxiation and*

sometimes death; death to energy and all
growth."
-- Horace Fletcher

The leader who seeks after what is good, righteous, just, holy, and equitable does so in all phases of life, whether in the office, the home, the church, or on the sports field. The leader seeks what is good for other departments in the organization, even if it means that the leader's own department must give up something to improve the life of another. The righteous leader understands the spiritual Laws of Reciprocity, Unity, and Greatness (Robertson, 1992) and is the type of leader from whom other department heads seek information and advice. This leader is the person who most often can speak at a meeting and bring peace to the table.

Let's take a look of some of these leaders. This story has two purposes, first to illustrate that sometimes a leader doesn't fully understand the *"why"* of a situation, and second, that followers who work with a righteous leader learn to trust the leader's judgment since the leader always seeks what is right. I knew of a situation where a leader decided that she had to hire three people for the organization that she led. (Her decision was met with frustration and argument by three of her four direct reports, because they thought that the newly hired people were not necessary, that they would only drain resources, and that the new employees would hamper existing operations.

Eight months later, the organization announced a merger that was not previously known to this leader, and the organization's president put her in charge of the new merger. The three employees had specific skills that were needed in the newly merged entity, and since the three employees were already familiar with the organization, the merger went smoothly and the new blended operation produced more benefit for the organization than previously estimated.

Sometimes seeking what is right requires the trust of followers, but since we have three prior Beatitudes that contribute to trust, it seems logical that the *agapao* leader would not have to worry about trust.

It is not as difficult to attain this Beatitude, as it might seem on the surface. Note, the Beatitude says that if the leader truly seeks after that which is good, right, holy, just, and equitable, he will be filled. The use of the verb form "will be" is future-present tense meaning that it is an activity that must follow another. If you truly seek what is good, you will receive it. Simple, isn't it?

Beatitudes Working Together

The Beatitudes work together to show us what a "whole" or complete leader looks like, and Aaron Feurstein, owner of Malden Mills, is an example of both the Beatitude of "seeking what is right" and the Beatitude of "mourning for those around him." In December of 1995, the Malden Mills textile mill burned to the ground leaving 2,400 people out of work. This loss of jobs and payroll would have caused a serious problem for the town of approximately 40,000 people, but Ferustein did the right thing, the just thing, the holy thing, and Feurstein paid all of his employees their full pay for three months while the firm rebuilt the mill. Some of the 2,400 employees were working right away in the clean up and rebuilding efforts, but no one lost pay.

One can only wonder how Adam Smith would have interpreted this? In an article in the *Christian Science Monitor*, Feurstein is quoted as saying, "There's some kind of crazy belief that if you discard the responsibility to your country, to your city, to your community, to your workers, and think only of the immediate profit, that somehow not only your company will prosper but the entire economy will prosper as a result . . .[BUT] I think it's dead wrong."

What were the results of Feurstein's actions? Well, Adam Smith would claim that the adage of the butcher and brewer was right – the mill's production doubled from what it used to be and the reject rate was cut in half. But Feurstein didn't seek what was right because of his future gains. Feurstein was 70 years old at the time and would have done better financially to take the insurance money and retire somewhere in the southern states. Retirement would have been the self-interest thing to do, but Feurstein sought the right thing because *it was the right thing* to seek.

Selah

How are you doing lately when it comes to seeking what is right, just, or holy? When an opportunity seems to present itself, are you thinking about the value of the opportunity or are you thinking about the value to you?

If your organization's senior leader asks you to consider a joint venture, do you look at both sides of the deal or just your own? What do you do if you want to protect both parties, and your senior leader asks you to get more for your own firm?

Do you feel a sense of injustice and certain behaviors in your organization? The *agapao* leader who follows this Beatitude does something about the injustice. Does this describe you? Or do you follow the Beatles' song – "Let it Be?"

Chapter 6: The Value of Mercy in a World that seems to Lack Mercy

Blessed are the merciful, for they will be shown mercy.

This Beatitude focuses on the Law of Reciprocity (Robertson, 1992), meaning that if you are merciful you will be shown mercy. The Greek word used here, *eleemon*, translates equitably into English as *"compassionate"* or *"merciful."* So, in this case, English is not a barrier to understanding the meaning of the Beatitude. There are two interesting aspects of the use of *eleemon*. The first is that it is an active tense. The leader must be merciful in the current sense of the word. The second point of interest is that this word is only used one other time in the entire New Testament -- Hebrew 2:17says, *"...* a merciful and faithful high priest in service to God and that he might make atonement for the sins of the people."* Other forms of mercy such as *eleeo* do occur elsewhere in Scripture. Shakespeare wrote that *". . .* mercy seasons justice,"* and this is the essence of this Beatitude to the leader. Mercy implies that an understanding heart is applied to the situation of judgment.

From the online Encyclopedia of Self, mercy is defined as "Forbearance to inflict harm under circumstances of provocation, when one has the power to inflict it; compassionate treatment of an offender or adversary; clemency" (http://www.selfknowledge.com/59113.htm). This definition seems to connect with the Beatitude of controlled discipline and helps illustrate how The Beatitudes work together.

To further understand mercy, it might be helpful to see mercy as being related to, but different than justice and grace. Mercy is NOT getting what you deserve, while justice

63

is getting what you deserve, and grace is getting what you don't deserve. All three are important in the relationship with other people as well as in our relationship with God.

Human justice is rough and blundering, full of rules and regulations. There seems to be little regard for the person or for the long-term learning that might come out of a situation that demands mercy. Mercy commands that the leader first examine the heart of the employee. The leader must consider if the employee saw an action as wrong, or if the employee was unaware of the consequences of the behavior. If the employee confesses the wrong action and shows repentance (a turning away from the action) then the leader must show mercy in his judgment. Why, you ask? Because the focus of correction is *"correction"* and not vengeance. If repentance is shown, then the first major step for correction has occurred.

Comparing the Value of Mercy with the Gift of Mercy

I find it interesting that of all the Beatitudes, this one is the only one that ties directly to the Spiritual gifts recorded in Romans 12, with one subtle difference, perhaps not in meaning, but in application. The Beatitudes are values held by a person, whereas the gifts in Romans 12 are more like capabilities. In Romans 12, the Greek word that we find for mercy is *eleeo*, which infers having compassion. The intensity of the passage on Spiritual gifts implies an extraordinary capability or capacity. Perhaps the value of showing mercy, as referenced in this Beatitude, does not have to occur at an extraordinary level. In other words, the Beatitude of mercy is intended for all people while the gift of mercy is intended for a few people.

Examples of Mercy from Scripture

Matthew 18:26-35 tells the vivid story of a young man who received forgiveness of a debt, and then was dealt with harshly with after he showed no mercy to those who owed him money. You see, God forgives us our sins when we come to Him seeking forgiveness and demonstrating repentance. I am grateful that He does, for many of my past actions deserve stiff punishment.

We see in the story of the prodigal son (Luke 15:11-31) how a leader exhibits the Beatitude of mercy when his son took his inheritance early and went off and squandered it. When the son came home penniless, the father had every imaginable right to tell his son to go away, but he didn't. In fact, he was so overjoyed that his son had returned to him, that he welcomed him back and had a celebration in his honor. What a picture of God's mercy toward us! The mercy on the father's part was made possible because the son was truly repentant; he was sorry for his misdeeds, and he completely desired to be reunited with his father.

You see, mercy allows us to forgive and to forget that which is not necessary for the future. Contrast this situation with a situation in which an atheist leader offended an employee who happened to be a Christian. When the employee commented on her feelings, the atheist leader responded, "You're a Christian, so you must forgive me as many times as I offend you. I've got it easy, you've got it hard. Ha!" The atheist failed to realize that repentance must come before forgiveness, and that right actions must follow forgiveness. Mercy does not mean accepting another person walking on or abusing you.

65

Recounting a Time when Mercy begat Mercy

A few years ago, I was involved in a situation that allowed me to see firsthand how this Beatitude works. I was in the early stages of learning about *agapao* leadership and was trying to practice what I was learning. One afternoon I got a call from the ethics committee chairman at the university. The chairman informed me of an allegation regarding one of my employees and a graduate assistant who worked for us. The employee and graduate assistant had allegedly violated university rules of ethics and the graduate assistant had gained access to students' grades. I assured the chairman that I would look into this and within an hour I had all the facts. Indeed, the graduate assistant had gained access to a secured area of the university's database and the employee had assisted the student. The graduate assistant was a student of another school on campus and had completed his course of study and was waiting to learn if he had passed all of his courses for the last semester, which would then allow the student to move on to post-graduate work. The school he was attending was not known for notifying students of passing/failing grades, and allowed the university grade notification system to notify the students. This required a three-week wait after final exams and the wait was creating considerable stress on the students.

The graduate assistant, feeling anxious about the outcome of his final exams, asked the employee who worked with me to allow the student to look at the official database of grades. The employee, understanding the anxiety that the student was experiencing, felt compassion for the student and allowed the student access to his computer, which was already logged into the database. The student ended up not only looking up his own grade, but also that of another close friend who was in the same situation. I discussed this set of actions with both the employee and the graduate assistant and it was clear to me that their motives were based on trying to help other people. Both realized that if they had come to me and had asked, I would have arranged to get the information through the correct channels. Both acknowledged that their behaviors were inappropriate, and pledged to me not to do it again.

I called the chairman of the ethics committee and explained what I had learned and that I was comfortable that their motives were good and that the behaviors would not occur again. Later that week, I heard that a small group of people on campus was calling for the dismissal of the employee. I then spent a fair amount of time over the next few weeks defending the employee and convincing people that he should not be dismissed. But that is just one side of the lesson. About six months later, I unknowingly did something that placed that same employee in a very poor light with students, such that my actions could have even possibly resulted in a defamation claim. My actions were not meant to harm him, and I was not aware of the extremely negative results. The employee could have brought me up on ethics charges! The employee, however, remembered that I had shown him mercy six months earlier, and he showed me mercy in exchange. The matter ended and we both continued to work together for many years. Mercy begat mercy!

Mercy Improves Communication

Working for a leader who exhibits the related Beatitudes of controlled discipline and mercy improves communication as well as organizational performance. How awful to work in an organization where people are accused of wrongdoing and who are punished for each transgression. Employees in these environments tend to write numerous memos to protect themselves and to deflect any anger stemming from the leader. In addition, employees tend not to take risks, since risks increase the likelihood of failure and failure leads to punishment. Finally, if an actual problem does arise, no one wishes to admit guilt. If no one admits guilt, either the punishment is spread across many people or no one gets punished at all. Sort of like the prisoner's dilemma game.

I recall some time ago, when I came to work one Monday morning and found that the school's student database was nowhere to be found on the network computer drives. The file was there, but no data! The school maintained this separate database in addition to the university's database for tracking of school-specific information. This occurred during my early days of studying *agapao* leadership and trying to behave like an *agapao* leader. I asked everyone in the office if anyone knew what had happened. No one did, or at least, no one would say. For hours I scoured the network drives and talked at length with our network support people. Then, late in the afternoon, one of the employees came to my office and told me that she was sure that she had caused the problem. She had to work over the weekend and chose to take Saturday off and to work on Sunday evening. When she was in the office she used the database and recalled seeing an unusual question come up on the computer screen when she logged out.

My first instinct was to yell at her for destroying what would take days of work – her time – to rebuild. Even if we could get a back-up copy off of the network, we would not know all of the edits that had occurred and would have to check each record to see if changes were needed. Instead, I decided to behave like an *agapao* leader, even if I wasn't feeling like one at the moment. I asked her to recount for me all that she could remember, and it appeared to me that she had somehow highlighted the data table and hit the delete button. Further conversation indicated that she was trying to back out of the database and thought that she was just deleting the last command.

So, here we were with the situation of an employee meaning well and acting on behalf of the organization. At first, I couldn't believe that it would be so easy to delete the data from a database, so I built a database and entered 10 records of data. As I was exiting the database, I highlighted the table and hit the delete key. Sure enough, a short message appeared, and if I was in a hurry, I might have ignored it and hit the enter key, and my data would have been gone.

What was the punishment for this employee? Nothing. We held some training for the entire staff to show how easy it was to delete data and we looked at the various security measures that we could use in the database program to prevent a future deletion. We were able to locate a back-up copy of the file on the network drive that was only two days old, so it didn't take long to repair the lost data. What was the overall result of this situation? We never lost the data again, the employee still works with me and we still don't have anybody spending time writing memos or behaving in self-protecting ways. Who needs to protect themselves when the leader is merciful? Imagine what would happen in all of the United States corporations if employees stopped spending time and energy building protective trails of paper and started taking some risks to benefit the organization.

I tell all of the people that work with me that I will always protect them if they make a mistake, but I may ask them to do the task differently in the future. Through this and other experiences in trying to become an *agapao* leader, I have learned that innovation only comes at the discretion of employees. One way to encourage discretion is to not punish them for well-intentioned failure. Only mercy can do that.

What's it Like to Work for a Merciful Leader?

Imagine working for a merciful leader. You know that if you do wrong that you expect the leader to call you on the carpet for clarification and redress. You know this and appreciate the teaching. Proverbs contains many references to the wise person seeking and accepting reproof. As you enter the leader's office, you know that you can expect to receive a measure of mercy and compassion. Your intentions were good even if your behavior was misguided. Later, when the leader makes a mistake and causes you difficulty, you willingly forgive and administer a measure of mercy to him or her as well. Do you think that you might defend the leader to other employees because he took your side with his superiors? Most employees desire to work for a merciful leader and to willingly give mercy in return.

> O man, forgive thy mortal foe
> nor ever strike him blow for blow,
> For all the saints on earth that live
> To be forgiven must forgive,
> For all the blessed souls in heaven
> Are both forgivers and forgiven.

(Baker, 1963, p. 66)

Blessed is the leader who shows compassion and mercy to the people who work with him, for his employees show him an equal amount of compassion and mercy.

Selah

How's your mercy score? Ask one of your employees who will tell you what you need to hear, and then listen patiently.

The next time that something goes wrong in your organization and your first reaction is to blame someone, ask yourself how much of the blame that you take as the leader. I have found that many times, errors occur in an organization because the leader placed inappropriate demands on people, or didn't provide enough training and/or resources, or perhaps didn't explain the process well enough. Then, after you have accepted your portion of the responsibility, talk to the employee. Show mercy, train them, communicate with them, and over a long time, watch the improved results. Note: It takes a long time for employees to learn to trust and to show mercy – they have a lot of unlearning to do.

Chapter 7: The Value of Integrity and a Focused Purpose

Blessed are the pure in heart for they will see God.

Pure in heart speaks directly to the integrity of a leader. The Greek word *katharos*, used in this Beatitude, means to be clean, clear, or pure, with a similar implication as to being undefiled or unblemished. The intent is the same as the Greek word *amiantos*, referred to in 1 Peter 1:4, which translates as *"pure"* or *"undefiled."* The Greek word *kardia*, from which we get *"heart"* in this passage, also translates as *"thoughts"* or *"feelings"* (the mind). Thus, we can conclude that the leader should be clean and undefiled in his thoughts and feelings. Yet, this definition goes beyond the ability to act well, to behave, or to control our thoughts. It is not acceptable to have unclean thoughts and then simply to suppress them. The concept of pure is that there is *no contamination* at all. As an example, the Pharisees of Jesus' time tried to act pure while covering up their inequities, but Jesus exposed their true thoughts and feelings.

This is a tough request to present to leaders. Not only does God call leaders to be merciful, He also calls them to have only good thoughts, feelings, and attitudes about other people. If we look at this Beatitude beyond the limits of how leaders relate to followers, then we conclude that the workplace would be free of gossip and that departments would be free of feuds. We would tear down the walls that we have built and replace them with arches (Winston, 1998).

Another way of looking at this Beatitude is in reference to the focus of the leader, since the definition of pure can also be *"unmixed."* This Beatitude calls leaders to focus their attention on the mission of the organization, and to not be looking here and there.

The justification, or reward, for purity of heart as stated in the Beatitude, is grand, it is to see God. This Beatitude leads me to believe that only the pure of heart, those with integrity, those with a focus on God, will be able to see God. The leader can only see God if there is nothing between him and the Master. The leader may have other loyalties, but these loyalties must be subordinate to God. The leader must be single-minded and focused first on serving and loving God. To further understand this, consider that Kierkegaard said that purity of heart is *"to will one thing."*

It is difficult to apply action steps to this condition of purity of heart. David was frustrated with how to be pure in heart. He recorded his words in Psalm 51:6-11:

Surely you desire truth in the inner parts; you teach me wisdom in the inmost place.

Cleanse me with hyssop, and I will be clean; wash me, and I will be whiter than snow.

Let me hear joy and gladness; let the bones you have crushed rejoice.

Hide your face from my sins and blot out all my iniquity.

Create in me a pure heart, O God, and renew a steadfast spirit within me.

Do not cast me from your presence or take your

Holy Spirit from me.

Restore to me the joy of your salvation and grant me a willing spirit, to sustain me. (NIV)

The first step to gaining a pure heart is to ask God for assistance. The reason to ask is that leaders are humans subject to all the frailties and faults of humankind. To be pure of heart is a challenge that no leader can achieve alone. The help of the Holy Spirit is crucial to the leader in becoming pure in heart, just as you can only know God with God's help. The good news is that God desires this for you, just as you desire it for yourself, so if you seek it, you will be on your way to finding fulfillment.

Keep the "Main Thing" the "Purpose."

Steven Covey coined the saying *"the main thing is to keep the main thing the main thing,"* and since Covey's book, *The Seven Habits of Highly Successful People,* the saying has been the focus of other books, sermons, speeches, etc. Why is this saying so popular? Because it is so right. I taught a course on the principles of marketing for many years and I encouraged – sometimes begged – students, as they were building their marketing plan, to spend the majority of the time developing the purpose section. The organization's purpose and thus, the leader's purpose/focus is what can and should drive the organization to great accomplishments. A good purpose statement should truly state the *"main thing"* and it should stimulate excitement in both the customers and employees.

As an example of what I am talking about, I offer the purpose statement of Merck pharmaceuticals as an excellent example.

"We are in the business of preserving and improving human life. All of our actions must be measured by our success in achieving this."
-- Merck's 1989 Statement of Corporate Purpose

Consider the purpose, "preserving and improving human life." There is nothing in this statement that says how or what the firm does. It does not say that the firm produces pharmaceuticals or anything else. Whatever the firm chooses to do must be in line with this purpose. If you were an employee of Merck, would you be motivated to work each day because the purpose of the firm was to make pills, or because your actions preserved and improved human life? If you are like most people, you would choose the latter.

Many employees are disassociated from their firm's mission because they cannot relate to what the firm says about its purpose. Few employees can get excited because a firm seeks to increase shareholder value, or trying to produce the highest quality tires, etc. A local pastor once commented in his sermon, "facts satisfy the mind, but passion excites the soul." That's it! A good purpose statement excites the soul. When you think about your purpose statement, be critical with yourself. After reading your purpose statement out loud, ask yourself: "Who cares?" If you cannot answer this question passionately, work on your purpose statement again, and again. A former student of mine wrestled with the issue of "who cares?" for his own firm. He worked for a regional environmental testing laboratory in the Northeastern United States. His first purpose statement talked about conducting tests, his second talked about helping environmental firms do better work, his third talked about improving the environment, and his last was "improving the health of all United States Citizens." His mission statement went on to talk about how his firm used environmental testing to help companies operate with a cleaner environment, thus improving health for all. For the first time since he started working with the firm, he got excited about what his firm did to improve the world in which he lived! If you're not excited about your firm, something ought to change, because if you aren't excited about your "main thing" it is hard to keep it the main thing.

Go Tell It On The Mountain.

When you know what your main thing is, it is the only thing that you should do. The world is full of great ideas, but if the idea that comes to your mind isn't part of your main thing, then ignore it. To help the employees and customers of your organization understand the unblemished pure focus of your heart – tell them, and tell them often! I have talked to many leaders who did not know their company's purpose, and there was not much that I could do to help them except to take them through exercises that would help to focus their thinking. But by far, the hardest for me to watch, are the leaders that articulate the unblemished focus of their companies, but keep the good news to themselves. When you know your focus – go tell it on the mountain! If every leader of every organization developed a good purpose statement and made sure that every advertisement emphasized the purpose, I promise you that advertising effectiveness would increase. Look back at the Merck purpose statement and ask yourself if you would want to work with a firm that sought to preserve and improve human life? I know I would! I wonder if Adam Smith would – or would he prefer to focus on increasing shareholder wealth?

Leaders need to continually put the vision and mission (related to the purpose) in front of followers. The leader that I work for travels extensively, and when she is back in town she likes to attend the staff meetings. She always asks me what I want her to cover, and my answer is the same every time; state the purpose and the mission of our school again.

Employees cannot hear the purpose and vision too many times.

Another benefit of repeatedly telling people your focus is that you won't forget it or allow other extraneous ideas to compete with it. Too often we get distracted and chase after the short-term benefits of wild hare ideas. When we do this, we forego the greater long-term benefits that we could enjoy if we paid more attention to the *"main thing."* This is the focus of the passage, Deuteronomy 11:18-25, in which Moses advises the people of Israel to focus on the Word of God, to keep the Word before them and to write the law on the door posts and the gates and to teach the children. It seems to me that the purpose of the organization and the purpose of the leader should be posted in the organization, so that followers, customers, suppliers, etc., see the words coming and going from the building.

The Tyranny of the "Good Idea."

Occasionally I am called in as a consultant to discuss a *"good idea"* with an organization's leadership. After listening to the good idea, I am asked to give my opinion as to whether this is something the organization should pursue. While I am glad to participate in this type of exercise, it is usually not a productive one. If the folks in the organization would only review the purpose of the organization and the leader, the decision would be obvious to them. If they would ask if the idea fits the purpose of the organization, they would have their answer. If it doesn't fit, then ignore it or give it to some other organization, even if it could be the next replacement to the microwave oven. If you want your company to be the one to create the replacement for the microwave oven, then start a new organization, but don't confuse the purpose of your first organization.

There are a million good ideas floating around. Sadly, some
ideas are rejected before anyone can evaluate the potential of
the idea to see how it fits the organization. While there are
many failed ideas, there are also a few incredible successes
such as Federal Express, in which a good idea took quite a
while to become a reality. We see this same relevance to
purpose and focus in organizations that try to diversify.
When companies diversify along the lines in which they
have already been successful, the organization obviously has
a greater chance of success. For example, if a fast food
company diversified into making movies, the probability of
success would be quite low since the success factors are
quite different. However, it seems logical that if a fast food
company diversified into a 10-minute oil change business,
the probability of success would be high, since the same
success factors of advertising, location, operations, customer
throughput, etc., are the same. The holding company of both
the fast food company and the oil change company would
have a purpose that was common and overarching to both
firms.

But, Pure in Heart is More than Purpose.

Now let's take a look at what this Beatitude means to be
undefiled in thought. The leader who is pure in heart would
never over react to seeing a *60-Minutes* camera crew waiting
outside the office. If you only think of good things, then you
will only do good things, except for the occasional mistake,
and mistakes do happen. It is not the mistake itself that gets
some people into trouble, but the cover up of the mistake. If
you only think good things, then you'll think enough to own
up to the mistake and it won't need to be covered up. Is this
a Pollyanna view? Perhaps just a little, given the number of
people whose behavior is the opposite of this Beatitude. But,

I have observed this kind of honesty at work. I have shared these lessons from The Beatitudes with many groups of people. In one of these seminars, I asked people to tell me if they worked for a boss who represented the characteristics of The Beatitudes. Usually, I find that one or two people out of twenty-five work for someone who portrays three of the Beatitudes. But it is rare to find employees who recognize more than three of the Beatitudes in their leader. In this seminar, as we discussed each Beatitude, I found two people who truly believed that their boss lived out each Beatitude. Curious about this, I asked if I could meet their boss. A month or so later, I received an invitation to present the seminar, *"Be a Leader for God's Sake,"* to the department where this *agapao* leader worked.

When I arrived, I met this leader and was convinced after a few minutes, that he probably did live up to all of the Beatitudes. This particular department provided a service to the organization (anonymity is kept here as a courtesy to the people involved) that was known in the industry to be a high-turnover, high-stress type of profession. Yet, I found out that most of the people in this department had been with the department for over five years and that twenty percent had been there at least ten years. These numbers reflected astounding staying power in an industry that averaged less than one year.

During and after this same seminar, I asked if these employees' leader had ever made mistakes. The answer was an overwhelming *"yes"* followed by, *"but we love him anyway."* In probing this response, I learned that this leader did, in fact, make mistakes. Lots of them! But, because his heart was so pure, his employees always knew that he never meant to harm anyone, and usually the leader discovered the

79

mistake before anyone else did, and he announced it himself. The employees commented that they had learned what their leader's weak spots were and where he usually made mistakes. So they just made sure that someone else did those activities, thus improving the success rate of the leader. This does not mean that the leader was inept -- he was far from it!

When your motives are obvious to everyone, people don't suspect you of doing wrong. When you know that your motives are pure, you can engage in more activities with a more relaxed approach, thus reducing stress and accomplishing more.

Selah

How are your motives?

If a *60-Minutes* film crew was waiting for you at the office, would you be nervous? What would you assume they wanted you to tell them? Do you have something to hide?

As part of your next performance review, ask your subordinates to conduct an anonymous review of you and ask them to comment on your credibility, integrity, and pureness of heart. What do you think you will find?

Focus on having pure thoughts. The benefits are incredible.

Chapter 8: The Value of Making and Keeping Peace

Blessed are the peacemakers, for they will be called sons of God.

In American society, the word peacemaking conjures up all kinds of mental images, everything from '60s peace signs to contemporary musicians joining hands and singing, *"We are the World."* But the Beatitude that we are talking about now is something much different, and it has direct implications for today's leaders.

The Greek word *eirenopoios*, as used here, is the word for *"peacemaker."* This word derives from *eirene* meaning *"one, peace, quietness, and rest"* and *poieo* meaning *"to make or do."* A leader must be one who causes peace, who causes quietness and rest in the workplace. This is very different from the image that most leaders project. Imagine working for a leader who strives to maintain a sense of peace and rest in the workplace! Now, don't make the mistake of thinking that this is a slow, dull work environment. There is great speed in the movement of a hummingbird's wings and a fast motion to its flight, yet when you watch the small bird, there appears to be great peace at the same time. You can experience a similar physical sensation by visiting a large aquarium. Many major cities maintain large aquariums with gigantic holding tanks. The big fish swim with strength and speed, and yet there seems to be a sense of peace and tranquility in their movements, a sense of harmony and unity.

The essence of this Beatitude is that the leader must seek to build and sustain unity in the workplace. Note, I used the two verbs, build and sustain. In Genesis, the Hebrew word

81

for create is *bara* and implies a formative condition -- to create and to sustain. By building and sustaining unity, the leader sets a condition in the workplace where strife cannot gain a foothold.

Just think of how much time and effort we waste suffering from extreme conflict or from trying to resolve it. Millions of legal cases backlog our court systems, each seeking judicial resolution for severe or perceived conflict. It seems that we have become a conflict-seeking people. How much more could we do if we were able to channel all this misplaced energy and wasted resources into feeding the hungry, healing the sick, and educating children?

Peace Begins with Peace.

Peacemakers are rare. To build and sustain unity requires humility, wisdom, knowledge, mercy, and purity in heart. Does this sound familiar? Re-examine the last three Beatitudes and review the characteristics of each. To make and sustain peace is an exacting, labor-intensive process. Peace does not occur because we do nothing. Peace is not an absence of strife. Peace is something that we maintain.

To be a peacemaker, the leader must first make peace in his own life before he can successfully make peace in his organization. A leader in conflict with himself is a house divided. Jesus spoke of a divided house in Matthew 12:25. Jesus knew the thoughts of the people that stood before Him and said to them, *"Every kingdom divided against itself will be ruined, and every city or household divided against itself will not stand."* When there is spiritual unity in the heart of the leader, then and only then, can he expect to create and sustain peace in the organization.

Peace is Fragile.

Peace does not sustain itself. Peace is a classic view of a system, and according to systems theory, a characteristic of a system is entropy, the slow self-destruction of a system. Thus, a leader has to continually intervene to maintain peace. You know the adage that says one bad apple can spoil the whole bunch. In this same way, a little strife ruins a peaceful organization. This means that a leader has to intervene in situations where someone creates strife.

People Migrate to Where There is Peace.

I recall observing an organization quite some time ago (anonymity is kept here out of respect for the people involved) that was full of strife. The leader did not live by The Beatitudes and used the organization for his own gain. His secretary and all of the telephone sales people had similar physical characteristics; they were female, blond, and beautiful. You get the picture. The leader constantly lied to the shareholders, to the board of advisors, to suppliers, and to the employees. As if this wasn't enough to cause frustration, he ordered his secretary and several of his direct reports to lie for him – with the exception of one person – a department head to whom a friend of mine reported. I had been hired as a temporary computer skills trainer and had the opportunity to observe the organization. One day my friend returned to her office to find another employee from another department crouched down in a sitting position between a couple of file cabinets. Startled, my friend asked the visitor what she was doing there. The visitor begged my friend to let her stay there for a while and not to tell anybody. The visitor explained that the organization was so stressful that the only place where there was peace was in my friend's department. You see, my friend's boss lived by The Beatitudes and created an oasis of peace in an otherwise strife-filled and frustrating organization.

Behaviors Don't Exist for Long when Values aren't Present.

Why then don't we see people in the world gravitating toward peace? We see the Middle East and countries in Africa trying to get along, but the basic values are not there to support the behaviors. On a past trip to Africa, I spoke with a person whose village was in conflict with another. I asked why the two villages were fighting, and my acquaintance told me that three generations ago there was a fight between members of the two villages and that one person killed the other. I asked who had killed whom and learned that no one remembered. If you don't have *agapao* love for someone, it is impossible to behave like you do for very long. If you don't care about people, as the second Beatitude says, and if your heart is not pure, as the sixth Beatitude requires, then it is certainly going to be hard to behave in ways that generate peace. Unfortunately, some people like to stir up strife; to them it is a form of power. Sadly for many, they just don't understand that they can say "no" to this type of behavior.

In my younger days, I remember studying psychology and reading with amazement how researchers placed participants at the controls of a panel that would administer an electrical shock when a person answered a question incorrectly. The person giving the answer was part of the experiment and never got more than a light shock, but pretended to receive ever-increasing doses of electricity. The real subjects of these experiments were the people who had the task of administering the shocks. After each session, the researchers asked the shock-givers how they felt. Most didn't like the experience and felt high levels of stress during the shock-administering role. Why then did these people administer the shock? Because they thought they had to.

If someone who is participating in a short psychological experiment is afraid to say *"No,"* and afraid to stop behaving in ways that cause harm to others, how much more pressure is on employees who are afraid of losing their jobs? It is sad to me that as Christians, we can say that we trust in Christ and offer our lives to Him, but we can't offer our jobs. I learned how to avoid this many years ago, long before my study and effort to become an *agapao* leader. I listened to a speech in which the presenter suggested that you need to give up your job the very first day you get it. The presenter suggested that we, as audience members, write a letter of resignation and sign it, but leave the date empty and give it to the boss with the instructions that he can, at any time, write in the date and have a clean dismissal. The next time that I started a job, I did and found the experience to be incredibly scary. The boss was shocked, too, and wasn't too sure that he had hired the right person!

Later on though, when the boss pressured me to do things that would have resulted in undue pressure on other people, I was quite comfortable saying *"No,"* but worked out other means of achieving the boss' expectations. This, I think, is similar to the account in the first chapter of the Book of Daniel when Daniel refused to eat the meat and wine of the king and sought another way to satisfy the concerns of Melzar. Daniel did not have to conform to please the king; he was able to say *"No."*

Is a Peacemaker a Pacifist?

What about the idea of war? Is the *agapao* leader a pacifist? No, the *agapao* leader does not avoid battle nor does he avoid confrontation when it is necessary. The *agapao* leader creates an environment in which peace can grow and flourish, but he is also ready to fight when needed. In the next section of this book, we will see the behaviors of retaliation and fighting addressed in more detail.

Peace is not the absence of conflict, but it is the manner in which conflict is addressed. In the leader's organization there will be times of conflict, but when the leader, and hopefully the followers, live by the first six Beatitudes, the resolution of conflict is swift and easy. In this way, it is similar to the passage in Ephesians chapter 5 about husbands and wives.

> *Submitting yourselves one to another in the fear of God.*
>
> *Wives, submit yourselves unto your own husbands, as unto the Lord.*
>
> *For the husband is the head of the wife, even as Christ is the head of the church: and he is the saviour of the body.*
>
> *Therefore as the church is subject unto Christ, so [let] the wives [be] to their own husbands in every thing.*
>
> *Husbands, love your wives, even as Christ also loved the church, and gave himself for it;*
>
> *That he might sanctify and cleanse it with the washing of water by the word,*

That he might present it to himself a glorious church, not having spot, or wrinkle, or any such thing; but that it should be holy and without blemish.

So ought men to love their wives as their own bodies. He that loveth his wife loveth himself.

For no man ever yet hated his own flesh; but nourisheth and cherisheth it, even as the Lord the church:

For we are members of his body, of his flesh, and of his bones.

For this cause shall a man leave his father and mother, and shall be joined unto his wife, and the two shall be one flesh.

This is a great mystery: but I speak concerning Christ and the church.

Nevertheless let every one of you in particular so love his wife even as himself; and the wife [see] that she reverence [her] husband.

Ephesians 5:21-33

We husbands like to read the one verse about wives submitting and we want to stop there. The whole passage implies that husbands have to make all decisions with the wife's best interest in mind. Who wouldn't want to submit when the other person makes decisions based on your best interest in mind? Do you want peace? Then consider the other person first.

Selah

How peaceful is your organization? Any strife or frustrations in the air?

Would I get the same answer if I asked your employees?

What might you do to increase the level of peace in your organization?

Over the next week, ask your employees and fellow co-workers about what they think about the level of peace in the organization.

Chapter 9: Summarizing the Beatitudes and Preparing for the Next Section

Blessed are those who are persecuted because of righteousness, for theirs is the kingdom of heaven

Blessed are you when people insult you, persecute you and falsely say all kinds of evil against you because of me

Rejoice and be glad, because great is your reward in heaven, for in the same way they persecuted the prophets who were before you

These next verses seem to reflect one overarching characteristic – the suffering of persecution. The word righteousness, which happens to be the same word used in the fourth Beatitude – *dikaisoune*, is a call to commitment. A leader who commits to integrity and to seeking that which is right(eous), holy, good, and equitable must stand for what he believes. To not be willing to take this stand for your commitment negates the value of the ethical statements.

But why suffer persecution? *Agapao* leaders will be successful and this success will be interpreted by other leaders as a threat, and their reaction will be to try to destroy the work of the successful leader, or to level the playing field.

I have experienced this type of persecution firsthand as a result of the *agapao* leadership style, and as a result have invested more time buffering my staff from the rest of the organization so that we could all concentrate on the tasks at hand. But I can also tell you that, in spite of the persecution, the gains are worth far more. So how does one prepare for this persecution? There are a variety of reactions that one might consider when faced with conflict: (a) retreat and abdicate one's values and behaviors to match the persecutor's values and behaviors, (b) defend one's behaviors and accept the persecution, or (c) quit.

The first alternative denies the truth and the importance of The Beatitudes. The third may allow you to be an *agapao*-leader in another organization. But the second option, defending one's behavior, is where I want you to focus.

How does one defend one's behaviors? An excellent example of defending one's behavior is found in the Old Testament when Daniel defended his decision not to eat the meat that was sacrificed to idols. Daniel knew he was not to eat meat sacrificed to idols and that he could refuse and not find a solution or he could stand on his principles and seek to show that his solution could be beneficial for the organization in the long run. Most organizations are results-oriented and the success or failure of a group, department, division, or larger entity, provides a base for evaluation. *Agapao* leaders are willing to show that their operations will perform well over the long term. When challenged on your *agapao* leadership style, ask to be allowed some freedom in your choices and to be able to measure the long-term performance. Your group's productivity should increase, their morale should increase, turnover should decrease, and overall job satisfaction should increase.

If you are not given the freedom to operate in all The Beatitudes, then see where you can make changes. In one organization, I was able to implement flextime and salary increases after redefining the job descriptions of the staff. The re-definition of the job descriptions came about as a result of my growing understanding of each person who worked in the department. Over time, the staff and I developed a good working relationship and I was able to

90

slowly implement more of the *agapao* principles into the workplace. Soon, the performance of the department reached a high enough level that other people in the organization noticed us. By this time, the performance was the focus of the attention and not the leadership style. By implementing the principles slowly, we built a positive reputation. Your decision to implement quickly or slowly will have to depend on how you believe other people in the workplace will view your behaviors.

Transitioning from principles to behaviors

In the Sermon on the Mount, Jesus presented The Beatitudes and then changed the focus from principles to examples and behaviors. In this book, I will present the second half of the Sermon on the Mount as a single chapter since each example is too short for a chapter of its own. As you read the information in the next chapter I encourage you to think about how each example that Jesus used can apply to your specific organizational setting.

Chapter 10: Applications from the Mountaintop

Salt and Light (You're a Christian, So Show It!)

> *Matthew 5:13-16: "You are the salt of the earth. But if the salt loses its saltiness, how can it be made salty again? It is no longer good for anything, except to be thrown out and trampled by men."*
>
> *"You are the light of the world. A city on a hill cannot be hidden. Neither do people light a lamp and put it under a bowl. Instead they put it on its stand, and it gives light to everyone in the house. In the same way, let your light shine before men, that they may see your good deeds and praise your Father in heaven."*

Jason Martin (1986) believes that when Jesus called His followers *"salt,"* that it was a statement of fact, not a calling to a higher place. In calling his followers *"salt,"* Jesus was articulating what everyone should have already known. Augsburger (1982) states that salt represents three vital qualities: (a) purity, (b) preservation, and (c) flavor. Believers are to have these qualities in order to be agents of change.

Today, most of us don't appreciate salt as the Hebrews and Romans did at the time when Jesus presented his lesson from the mount. You have to realize that in Jesus' day, soldiers often received their pay in salt (the root word is the same as *"salary"*). Don't let the limitations of the English language deprive you of the rich opportunity to grasp this truth. After all, we have so much salt that many of us are on salt-restricted diets! We even have salt substitutes. Salt was a rare and valuable commodity that was essential for preserving food and for adding flavor.

Jesus also called his followers to be the *"light of the world."* In our society today, we have a hard time valuing *"light,"* compared to the biblical era when the brightest household light was a candle. In the inner city we actually suffer from a condition called *"light pollution."* Many inner-city dwellers have not seen the grandeur of a starry night, and have to drive dozens of miles to get far enough away from the city to see a meteor shower. Pictures from the space shuttle reveal the eerie glow of urban streetlights on our planet at night. One can only wonder what would happen if Jesus gave this sermon today. Perhaps, instead of salt and light, we would have been called to be the "clean air" and "clean water" of the earth. Okay, I'm not going to rewrite Scripture, but I want you to consider the value and importance of *"salt and light"* to the people sitting on the mountainside listening to Jesus' words.

Earl Palmer (1986) helps us understand the value of salt by reminding us *"*[e]very listener in the first-Century Mediterranean world would be able to appreciate the importance of this salt image. The value of salt is tested not by the way it appears, but by what happens as a result of its use *"* (p. 30). As Christian leaders put more of their Christianity into the workplace, the more favorable and preserved the workplace becomes. However, if the Christian leader goes overboard in pushing his or her Christianity, the workplace can become too salty and will be unsuitable for consumption by fellow workers.

Consider the use of salt to flavor food. When a cook adds salt to a broth, the salt is no longer visible, but if sufficient salt has been used; the taste of the salt is clearly present.

However, if the cook continues to add too much salt to the broth, it is not likely that the broth will be good to the palate. On the other hand, when there is a need to preserve a food, such as meat, the amount of salt is increased to the point that the taste may be negatively affected, but the meat is still preserved and protected. Before consuming, the meat is usually soaked or otherwise treated to remove the excess salt.

There is a strong admonition given to those who wish to follow Jesus. Our Lord tells us that if a Christian loses his or her "saltiness," i.e., purity, or ability to preserve or flavor, then the only option is to be discarded. The New International Version of the Scriptures puts this passage this way, ". . . to be thrown out and trampled by men." In Luke 14:35, Luke states it this way: "It is fit neither for the soil nor for the manure pile; it is thrown out." The original Aramaic, according to Bowman and Tapp (1957), reveals a play on words. The Aramaic words for "ground" and for "dung" are *lara* and *lrea* that sound very much alike when pronounced.

Matthew's account in the King James translation of the Scriptures refers to "trodden" by man. The Greek word for trodden is *katapateo* meaning "to reject with disdain, or to be trampled underfoot." This is strong language, for it implies that if a Christian leader does not act as salt in the workplace by preserving and flavoring, then Christ will reject him. Since I follow the evangelical teachings that consider salvation as secure, then this passage implies that although salvation is secure, Christ will not be able to use the Christian to further His kingdom.

Pelikan and Cardman (1973), in their analysis of St. Augustine's teaching on the Sermon on the Mount, point out that this crucial admonition harkens back to the aforementioned Beatitude. Jesus warned His followers that they would receive persecution. St. Augustine added this to the salt analogy saying that the Christian must not be afraid to act from fear of persecution. For if he or she does fail to act, then what good can the Christian provide to the world.

Now let's dive into the virtues of Christians being "light." Leo Eddleman (1955) offers an excellent analogy for what Jesus was referring to in this Sermon on the Mount. Eddleman says: "Light warms as it radiates. Its life-giving quality sustains us physically on the earth. 'In Him was life: and the life was the light of men' (John 1:4). The light of God's love, warm and life giving, is the source of all religion that is not counterfeit. The word 'light' in New Testament language is the root for our word 'phosphorescent'; there is a continual glow" (p. 31). The Greek word Eddleman refers to is *phos* meaning to "shine or make manifest." Both are appropriate words to describe the Christian leader in the workplace. Because of the leader's Christian "light," it should be clear to all employees in the workplace that this person is indeed a Christian, but the light should not be so overpowering that those around the leader turn away.

Jesus went on to say that believers are "a city on a hill." This is a metaphor for the Christian leader to act as a guide for the sojourner. Imagine walking across a large plain at night. There ahead is a city set on a hill, with the city's lights visible for tens of miles. The city's lights act as a beacon to guide you to your destination. This is an excellent analogy for a Christian leader whether he or she is mentoring a younger employee or sharing the vision of the organization.

Jesus uses light as a multi-faceted symbol. He uses light to show illumination, or phosphorescence, and as a lighthouse

95

guiding the wanderers. And He uses light as a source of warmth and comfort. I lived many years in Alaska where the winters are cold, long, and dark. Many stores installed large heat lamps just inside the outer doorways that afforded the entering patrons a refreshing presence of warmth and light as they entered. The departing patrons enjoyed the same experience just before entering the frigid arctic air as they left the store. Coming and going, patrons received a welcome respite from the world's torment. Imagine the Christian leader, now, as a warm, comfortable respite in a tormented world. How much more could this Christian do for the kingdom than one who was dull and cold, indistinguishable from the worldly leaders that abound?

Jesus calls Christian leaders and supervisors to be both salt and light. This is a statement of "required" functional behavior. D. Martyn Lloyd-Jones (1962) said it well:

> *"I suggest to you, therefore, that the Christian is to function as the salt of the earth in a much more individual sense. He does so by his individual life and character, by just being the man that he is in every sphere in which he finds himself. For instance, a number of people may be talking together in a rather unworthy manner. Suddenly a Christian enters into the company, and immediately his presence has an effect. He does not say a word, but people begin to modify their language. He is already acting as salt, he is already controlling the tendency to putrefaction and pollution. Just by being a Christian man, because of his life and character and general deportment, he is already controlling that evil that was manifesting itself, and he does so in*

every sphere and in every situation. He can do this, not only in a private capacity in his home, his workshop or office, or wherever he may happen to be, but also as a citizen in the country in which he lives."

Murder (Anger in the First Degree)

Matthew 5:21-26: "You have heard that it was said to the people long ago, 'Do not murder, and anyone who murders will be subject to judgment.' But I tell you that anyone who is angry with his brother will be subject to judgment. Again, anyone who says to his brother, 'Raca,' is answerable to the Sanhedrin. But anyone who says, 'You fool!' will be in danger of the fire of hell.

Therefore, if you are offering your gift at the altar and there remember that your brother has something against you, leave your gift there in front of the altar. First go and be reconciled to your brother; then come and offer your gift.

Settle matters quickly with your adversary who is taking you to court. Do it while you are still with him on the way, or he may hand you over to the judge, and the judge may hand you over to the officer, and you may be thrown into prison. I tell you the truth, you will not get out until you have paid the last penny."

When Jesus referred to the Commandment, saying, "Thou shalt not kill," he was directly challenging the day's interpretation of the law, but He didn't stop there, He added the clause "and anyone who murders will be subject to judgment." The original commandment was to not kill – no exceptions. With the addition of what would happen if you do kill, the statement ceased to be a commandment and became a law. In the second half of the Sermon on the Mount, Jesus sought to restore the commandments to a former higher calling (Lloyd-Jones, 1962, p. 222).

The word *"angry,"* that Matthew uses is the Greek word *argizo*. *Argizo* means, *"provoking or enraging another, to become exasperated, or to become angry with another."* This infers the need for patience. *Raca* is a word of disgust and disdain which one person might feel towards another. The word literally means an *"empty-one."* The phrase, *"You fool,"* comes from the Greek word *moros* meaning *"dull, stupid, heedless, or absurd."* Jesus instructs everyone to avoid even the thought of ill will toward another. Martin Luther King, in his work *Stride Toward Freedom*, admonished people *"to avoid not only violence of deed but violence of spirit."*

Augsburger (1982) wrote:

> *While one may say he has never killed, Jesus asks about the inner attitude of anger and hate, of destructive words and hostility. Anger wounds others and also warps the spirit of the one immersed in the feeling of wrath or indignation. We need to understand our feelings to be honest about them, but we must resolve anger in other ways than focusing on personalities with destructive attitudes toward them. Paul writes, 'If you are angry, don't sin . . . ' (Eph. 4:26). Anger is a temporary madness and its expression has no place in the community of disciples.*

Does this imply that the Christian leader or supervisor must not have angry thoughts? In other parts of the Scripture we see Jesus speaking poorly of the Pharisees and the moneychangers who were doing business in the inner walls of the temple. Note the example set by Jesus, though. In Jesus' anger, He is angry at injustice and the blindness of those who should be able to see.

Jesus' words in the Sermon on the Mount speak to being angry without cause. This is like the leader who sees an employee sitting for a moment and then becomes angry with the employee for slothfulness. There may be many reasons why the employee was sitting idly. The leader in this example violated Jesus' teaching by getting angry without cause. Jesus calls the Christian leader to understand the spirit of the commandment rather than the letter of the law.

Continuing with this thought, Lloyd-Jones (1962) wrote:

> *The holier we become, the more anger we shall feel against sin. But we must never, I repeat, feel anger against the sinner. We must never feel angry with a person as such; we must draw a distinction between the person himself and what he does. We must never be guilty of a feeling of contempt or abhorrence, or of this expression of vilification.* (p. 226)

Consider Matthew 12:34b: "For out of the overflow of the heart the mouth speaks." Also consider the Beatitude, "Blessed are the pure of heart." Jesus sees our heart as the place where we must block evil and prevent it from entering, for to think evil and to do good is hypocrisy. Jesus admonishes anyone who harbors ill will to literally go to that other person and to reconcile the differences. The word that we translate as "agree" comes from the Greek word *eunoeo* meaning, "to be well minded or reconciled." Jesus elevates His reconciliation directive to even greater heights by saying

99

that Christians should not sue their *"brothers."* The word
"brother" in Greek is *adelphos*, means a literal or figurative
brother. Jesus is saying that you will be better off by settling
with the one you have wronged than waiting and having the
matter tried before people who do not know you.

I wonder how many leaders who are caught embezzling,
engaging in insider trading, or conducting illegal corporate
espionage would be better off confessing their wrong-doings
to their CEO and negotiating a settlement rather than trying
to hide within the legal system by pleading not guilty. These
Scriptures indicate that the Christian leader who commits a
wrong against an employee or another leader must go to the
injured party, reconcile, and settle. It takes a mature leader to
admit that he or she is wrong and to offer physical or
emotional restitution. Accompanying this is, of course,
repentance.

Christian leaders should see from this passage that if they
harbor ill will toward an employee, then they must quickly
discuss the matter and not let it fester into a seething wound
of anger. Left to its own, anger soon becomes a tool for
Satan. Think of yourself or someone you know who became
angry with another person and allowed it to stew for a while
without dealing with it. If you are like most people, sooner
or later an explosive encounter occurs between the two
parties with harsh words that develop into emotional hurts.
How do you think the world would see a Christian leader in
this light? Certainly not as a beacon on the hill set there to
guide others!

The Abilene Paradox is a wonderful book filled with many
insights that seem to fit the Sermon on the Mount. One of the
essays in the book discusses a Japan Airlines pilot who,
through pilot error, landed six miles short of the runway at

the San Francisco airport, in the water. The passengers said that it was such a smooth landing no one realized that the plane was in the water until a boat passed by! Later, when the pilot, named Asah, entered his hearing to answer charges of poor performance, the pilot said, "Like Americans say – Asah *screwed* up" (the text of the conversation implies a harsher word here). No one could argue with the pilot since it was exactly as he said. At least he was honest. I can't help but wonder how President Nixon would have fared in the press had he followed the same line of action as this Japan Airlines pilot. I wonder what our court systems might look like if we all owned up to our actions.

Anger doesn't have to be "big anger," even "little anger" is included in this teaching by Jesus. After one year of studying and attempting to develop into an *agapao*-leadership style, I was particularly busy with a full pile of work on my desk. I walked out of my office to get some materials that I needed and I noticed my assistant talking with friends on the phone. I could always tell when she was talking with friends because the tone of her voice and the selection of words varied from when she was talking to other administrative staff or to her family. I thought to myself, "I hope she gets off the phone quickly so we can complete all this work!" If I was busy, I was sure everyone else was, too!

An hour later, I came out of my office for more materials, and my assistant was on the phone again, but with a different friend. I could feel my anger rising and I began to mutter to myself as I gathered the next round of materials for my slowly decreasing pile of work. This time I could not keep quiet. I interrupted her conversation and asked about a project that I had assigned her the day before. She answered that the project was complete and that she had sent it on to

101

the next administrative office. I went into my office and placed the materials on my desk and then went back to my assistant. I interrupted her phone call again and asked her about a second project. Her response, like the first, was that the project was done and had been shipped on along its administrative path. An hour later, I left my office to get a cup of coffee, and my assistant was no longer at her desk but was now at the coffee pot talking with a co-worker. My anger rose. I walked up to my assistant and asked her about a third project. Her answer, like the previous answers was the same. Then she asked me a question: *"Bruce, why are you asking me if these projects are done?"* I answered quickly that there was a lot of work to be done and that I was concerned. She responded that the only person in the office who was not caught up on work was me, in fact, and that she was convinced that I really didn't trust her. I stammered that it wasn't true, but the longer I stood there and thought about it, the more I realized that what she said was right. We had a commitment in the office that when we had a lot of work to do, that we worked hard, and if we were caught up, we enjoyed the time as we desired. I admitted to her that she was right. She then looked at me and said: *"Bruce, you learned something today!"* And with that, she turned and walked down the hall. I stood there realizing that like the main character in the book *The Flight of the Buffalo* I had just reverted back to my original buffalo nature and had crashed back to the prairie.

According to the Sermon on the Mount, my thoughts of anger and frustration were totally unjustified. But what do you do with justified anger? As we discussed earlier in the book, Jesus gives us an excellent example. In the account of Jesus chasing out the money changers and the sellers from the temple, we see Jesus acting out of righteous anger, but acting with controlled discipline.

Adultery (Sexual Harassment/Discrimination)

> *Matthew 5:27-30: "You have heard that it was said, 'Do not commit adultery.' But I tell you that anyone who looks at a woman lustfully has already committed adultery with her in his heart. If your right eye causes you to sin, gouge it out and throw it away. It is better for you to lose one part of your body than for your whole body to be thrown into hell. And if your right hand causes you to sin, cut it off and throw it away. It is better for you to lose one part of your body than for your whole body to go into hell."*

Jesus' message regarding adultery countermands traditionally held beliefs of the Jewish community. In this passage, the law talks about adultery, but Jesus condemns lust. How often do we read about the leader who lost his job or took early retirement because of a sexual harassment suit? Some might say that he didn't commit adultery, and they would be right but the problem still remains. The *spiritual law* talks about the danger of lustfulness, and many leaders have paid the price for breaking this spiritual law.

Augsburger (1982) says that the interpretation of the old law was directed at the married man, and that adultery referred to "marriage breaking," or the violation of a covenant. But, Jesus broadened the meaning to both married and single people who needed to respect other people in the highest regard.

Eddleman (1955) sheds more light on this passage by pointing out that Jesus refers to lust as coming from the heart of man. A man can only blame himself for this sin. Augsburger (1982) and Eddleman (1955) both agree that Jesus considered this issue to be one of great severity, one to be avoided at all costs. Eddleman (1955) contends "Christ did not call for actual mutilations of the body but rather mastery of it" (p. 54). It is obvious that Jesus was referring to men in this passage in order to emphasize the importance of the message to male leaders and supervisors, but naturally, women are not excluded from this teaching. I see this passage commanding leaders to control lustful thoughts toward employees. Sexual thoughts are powerful emotions and Jesus' teaching aims at bringing this emotion under control. Martin Luther said: "I cannot keep the birds from alighting on my head, but I can restrain them from making nests in my hair."

Oaths (You're as Good as Your Word)

> *Matthew 5:33-37: "Again, you have heard that it was said to the people long ago, 'Do not break your oath, but keep the oaths you have made to the Lord.' But I tell you, Do not swear at all: either by heaven, for it is God's throne; or by the earth, for it is his footstool; or by Jerusalem, for it is the city of the Great King. And do not swear by your head, for you cannot make even one hair white or black. Simply let your 'Yes' be 'Yes,' and your 'No,' 'No'; anything beyond this comes from the evil one."*

At the time that Jesus spoke these words, Augsburger (1982) explains, the Jewish community had developed a hierarchy of oaths making some statements more binding than others.

Jesus was instructing His listeners that they must be honest and forthright with an oath. Today, if we could trust what another person told us, do you think we would need all of the attorneys and the mounds of legal paper that our nation generates each year? Imagine what it would be like to work for a leader or supervisor who always supported and fulfilled what was promised to you. Imagine what it would be like to be a supplier to an organization where the leader's words were binding. There would be no contracts, no invoices. Is it possible? There are actually some firms that are working at this level of relationship. Jesus calls leaders and supervisors to be careful in what they promise and then to always fulfill what they promise, regardless of the cost. The King James translation uses the word communication. The Greek word for *"communication"* is *logos* meaning, *"something said"* (including the thought). The Greek words for *"yes"* and *"no"* are *nai* and *ov*, respectfully, which bring to mind a strong affirmative and strong negative condition with no room for interpretation of meaning. Jesus commands leaders and supervisors to make their commitment either yes or no. Remove the gray areas and speak clearly so that your employees and peers can understand your message and know exactly what to expect.

Along these same lines, Martyn Lloyd-Jones (1962) clarifies what Jesus meant when He said that no one should ever take an oath. Lloyd-Jones illustrates this referring to numerous occasions where God's people (Abraham, Isaac, Jacob, and Joseph of the Old Testament; and Paul of the New Testament) and God, Himself, took oaths. Lloyd-Jones concludes from Scripture that there are places and times for oaths when there exists a sense of solemnity and differentiation. Jesus forbids the use of oaths in ordinary conversation, for there is no need to take an oath about an argument. Jesus calls for simple veracity, the speaking of truth, in all ordinary communications, conversations and speech (pp.268-269).

In contrast to Lloyd-Jones, R. Govett (1984) believes Jesus was saying that no one should ever take oaths. Govett makes a strong case by asserting that the Christian who takes an oath comes under the law and not under grace. Still, it seems that if Govett were correct, Jesus would have had to explain away the serious oaths of the Jewish fathers: Abraham, Isaac, Jacob, and Joseph. Remember in the Sermon on the Mount Jesus presented a series of principles that all people should live by every day. These create the code of behavior for daily living. It seems logical from Jesus' teachings that we can conclude that He is addressing heart-issues in this passage, just as He addressed heart-issues in the preceding passages. He seeks to show that we should live our life for good, in our hearts, our heads, and in our behaviors. To just act righteously is not enough; Christian disciples must *be* righteous. Jesus did not forbid lusting after one's spouse (because in that context, the behavior is appropriate), nor from showing anger when the situation called for anger (again, the context is critical), and He does not say that disciples should not swear an oath when the context calls for it. Matthew records Jesus responding to a question under oath in Matthew 26:63-66:

> *But Jesus remained silent.*
>
> *The high priest said to him, "I charge you under oath by the living God: Tell us if you are the Christ, the Son of God."*
>
> *"Yes, it is as you say," Jesus replied. "But I say to all of you: In the future you will see the Son of Man sitting at*

the right hand of the Mighty One and coming on the clouds of heaven."

Paul swears an oath in Romans 9:1:

"I speak the truth in Christ -- I am not lying, my conscience confirms it in the Holy Spirit."

And again in 2 Corinthians 1:23:

"I call God as my witness that it was in order to spare you that I did not return to Corinth."

Consider Hebrews 6:16-20:

"Men swear by someone greater than themselves, and the oath confirms what is said and puts an end to all argument. Because God wanted to make the unchanging nature of his purpose very clear to the heirs of what was promised, he confirmed it with an oath. God did this so that, by two unchangeable things in which it is impossible for God to lie, we who have fled to take hold of the hope offered to us may be greatly encouraged. We have this hope as an anchor for the soul, firm and secure. It enters the inner sanctuary behind the curtain, where Jesus, who went before us, has entered on our behalf. He has become a high priest forever, in the order of Melchizedek."

In the Hebrews passage, God took an oath as a sign to His people. Thus, it seems to me that there must be an appropriate time to take an oath. The issue in this lesson is how others see the disciples' behavior.

Jesus' earlier lesson stated that disciples should be like *"a city on the hill"*? This current lesson on oaths goes hand-in-hand with this teaching. As *"a city on a hill,"* Christian leaders are out in the open for all to see. Christian leaders must not exaggerate, or allow people to exaggerate for them. For the world will judge Christians by what they say, what they do, and what they permit. And ultimately, what others think of Christian leaders they will also attribute to Christ.

An Eye for an Eye (Discipline)

Matthew 5:38-42: "You have heard that it was said, 'Eye for eye, and tooth for tooth.' But I tell you, Do not resist an evil person. If someone strikes you on the right cheek, turn to him the other also. And if someone wants to sue you and take your tunic, let him have your cloak as well. If someone forces you to go one mile, go with him two miles. Give to the one who asks you, and do not turn away from the one who wants to borrow from you."

Jesus refers to the Old Testament advice from Exodus 21:23-25:

But if there is serious injury, you are to take life for life, eye for eye, tooth for tooth, hand for hand, foot for foot, burn for burn, wound for wound, bruise for bruise;

And Leviticus 24:20

fracture for fracture, eye for eye, tooth for tooth. As he has injured the other, so he is to be injured.

In the Code of Hammurabi, we see similar messages, but in the Code of Hammurabi, punishments exceeded the crimes. For many people in that day, these passages became the "Law of Revenge" requiring, in Jewish custom, the immediate punishment of one who committed an infraction against another person. Jesus pointed out how the Scribes and Pharisees misinterpreted the Scriptures. The intent of the Exodus and Leviticus passages was to limit the punishment that one might mete out. Jesus sought to show the Jewish community that the law bound no one, but rather that He came to *fulfill* the law, which was a greater call to love one another. Thus, all should live according to love.

Jesus also called believers to resist evil. The Greek word for "resist" is *anthistemi* meaning "to stand against" or "to oppose," and the Greek word for "evil" is *poneros* referring to "mischief, malice, grievous, harmful, malicious, or wickedness." On this subject, some authors such as Lloyd-Jones believe that Jesus commands all disciples to not resist evil, but to maintain a pacifist position at all costs. This could not be true for it would violate many other parts of Scripture where Jesus admonishes us to resist the evil one and to control our emotions. Jesus, Himself, drove demons out of people and enabled the apostles to do likewise. If such a premise were true, why would God give us Ephesians 6:10-18 about preparing for battle against the prince of this world? Why would Jesus have driven the moneychangers from the temple? Jesus is the epitome of resisting evil! Look again at the Greek. Jesus shows that disciples must live life according to the *spirit of the law* and not the letter of the law. The letter of the law demanded revenge for every infraction. Individuals would take the law into their own hands and seek retaliation. How many feuds have developed because an individual's interpretation led to retaliation? This is how feuds escalate to war. I believe that this passage calls Christian leaders who have been hurt by someone to respond in the spirit of love rather than a spirit of revenge. You have heard of leaders and supervisors who live by the motto: "I don't get over it, I get even." What message does this behavior communicate to followers? Augsburger (1982) says:

> *"We must recall Jesus' words that the citizens of
> His Kingdom are like salt to the earth, light to the
> world and yeast in the loaf; the minority which
> influences the whole but never dominates it,
> which lives by the higher ethic of love even at the
> cost in one's own life of the way of the cross."*

Many times, evil people or leaders (*poneros*) will mistreat
those under them just to watch them react negatively. But
how does the evil person react when the victim doesn't
respond? He will soon give up and seek another victim.
There is a story (I doubt it is true, but it does illustrate the
point) about an old man that lived in a small run down house
just a block from a junior high school. Every afternoon, a
group of boys from the school would stop by the old man's
house after school and taunt the old man and call him names.
The old man would come outside and yell at the boys and
raise his cane at them. The boys would laugh mischievously
and run away satisfied with their success.

At the beginning of a new school year, the old man changed
his strategy. As expected, the boys stopped by the old man's
house and called him names. This time though, the old man
came out and waved hello to the boys from the porch. The
old man then said: "If you boys will come back tomorrow
and yell at me some more, I will give each of you one
dollar." With that he turned and went back into the house.

The next day the boys returned and fulfilled the man's
wishes. True to his word, the old man came out and gave
each of the boys one dollar. He waved to the group and said,
"See you tomorrow." Tomorrow came and so did the boys.
After the boys had yelled and taunted the old man, the old
man came out and said, "I cannot pay you a dollar anymore,
for all I have is a quarter for each of you. Please come back

tomorrow." The next day the boys, again, yelled and taunted the old man. The old man came out and said, "I can only pay each of you a dime, for I am nearly out of money."

With this, the leader of the group of boys said: "A dime? It's not worth it. Let's go guys." The boys left and never bothered the old man again. When the evil one (*poneros*) does not get the desired result, his behavior changes.

Let's now look at what it means to go "the extra mile." Let's consider the laborer who is required to work eight hours, but routinely works nine hours without request for more pay. Should the leader be expected to pay without being asked? If the leader is required to pay for eight hours of work, but instead pays for nine, should the worker come to expect that generosity? When we live by law, we also work and pay by law. This is the great sin of the economic world that Adam Smith laid out for us in his work *The Wealth of Nations*. Smith's call was for each person to pay as little as possible for as much gain as possible. This has become the great mantra of capitalism, but of course, it is incorrect. The greatest gains come from the greatest commitment of workers and followers, not by paying them as little as possible. Carnegie is credited with giving away 90 percent of his income near the end of his life and supporting all of the people that he could. He was quoted as saying that his gain came from what he gave, not from what he made. I agree that there are people who will take advantage of others who are so generous, but no leader is required to keep and build relationships with those who would do harm. The goal of *agapao* leadership is similar to the goal of transformational leadership in that both leader and follower seek to lift the other to higher levels. Like Carnegie, leaders

111

and followers who go the extra mile have the greatest chance
to influence those whom they serve.

Love Your Enemies (Competition)

> *Matthew 5:43-48: "You have heard that it was said,
> 'Love your neighbor and hate your enemy.' But I tell
> you: Love your enemies and pray for those who
> persecute you, that you may be sons of your Father in
> heaven. He causes his sun to rise on the evil and the
> good, and sends rain on the righteous and the
> unrighteous. If you love those who love you, what
> reward will you get? Are not even the tax collectors
> doing that? And if you greet only your brothers, what
> are you doing more than others? Do not even pagans do
> that? Be perfect, therefore, as your heavenly Father is
> perfect."*

I treat this passage separately because so many people see
this as a separate concept from the *"Law of Revenge"* that
we just discussed. I also treat this passage separately because
it is at this point that I part from the thinking of other writers
(Augsburger, 1982, Lloyd-Jones, 1962, Govett, 1984,
Eddleman, 1955).

I do agree with these other writers that this passage is a
continuation of the previous and that you will more fully
understand by reading the two as one long thought (Matthew
5:36-48). To set the stage for my explanation of this passage,
consider the following facts from Scripture. God already set
the rule of loving your neighbor in the Old Testament. Jesus
said this was the second greatest commandment. As a result,
the Israelites were supposed to treat each other well and to
not charge excessive interest, or to deny the wants of
another. The Old Testament also held strong language

regarding enemies, in fact, Exodus and Leviticus recommend destroying enemies in battle.

The question that the Israelites debated for centuries is Jesus' central theme. The Israelites learned from early childhood that their countrymen were their neighbors, while all non-Israelites were their enemies. Imagine growing up believing that someone who is different from you is your enemy. This sheds light on the Middle East struggles of today, doesn't it? The Israelites grew up believing that bigotry was a natural state of events. If someone came from Samaria, no Israelite would trust that person. Most likely, the Israelites would try to cast the Samaritan out of Israel.

This is why Jesus' story of the Good Samaritan, told in Luke 10:30-37, is such a shock to the Pharisee's question regarding just who is "a neighbor." Jesus intentionally uses a Samaritan, a person that most Israelites would have described as an enemy, to be the neighbor in His story. The thieves were not neighbors, the priest was not a neighbor, but the one to whom most Jews would not have given the time of day, was the neighbor.

Let me digress for a moment. The Winston family (the branch from which I am descended) settled in what is now southern Virginia and northern North Carolina during the 1670s. In the late 1990s, I met my father's cousin who still lived in northern North Carolina. During our visit, she recalled a conversation that she had with her great-grandmother in the early 1920s. My father's cousin was beginning to date and her great-grandmother wanted to give her some advice, and this is what she said, "Stay away from those Virginia boys because you know what they are like!" Imagine that just because you lived across a state line you were considered to be bad. I'm wondering just how much has changed since the time that Jesus spoke the Sermon on the Mount!

Many people see this passage as Jesus advocating a pacifist lifestyle. But this whole treatise, so far, has been to show the Israelites how they misunderstood God's laws. God commanded people to love their neighbor. Jesus showed the Jewish crowd that the spirit of this law abides in the heart. To hate someone whom you do not know, and who has committed no violation against you is simply wrong. Today, we call it bigotry.

To drive this home, let's consider some of the Greek language in this passage. The Greek word for "hate" is *miseo* that means to "detest" or "to love less." The word for "enemy" comes from the Greek *echthros* meaning "hateful, hostile, or adversary." Remember the passage on the Law of Reciprocity? If the Israelites hated people from other countries, it is only logical that people in other countries would hate them and would retaliate with equal, if not escalated, feelings and actions.

Jesus showed the Jewish community that their misinterpretation of the old laws led to hatred toward people they did not even know that resulted in a breakdown of relationships. Instead of hating, Jesus showed them that they should love their enemies. The Greek word for love here is *agapao,* the very basis for The Beatitudes!

Jesus stated in this passage that the spirit of the law called for people to naturally feel goodwill toward one another, even if the other person was a stranger. However, a quick reading of Jesus' comments to the Pharisees in the Gospels will dispel any belief of Jesus being a pacifist.

Of additional interest in this passage is the use of the Greek words for *"sons"* and *"brothers"* which are *huios* and *adelphos,* respectfully. Both words imply a distant or figurative kinship. Jesus did not speak about true sons or brothers, but rather that people should look upon those with whom they are interacting as if they were either their children or siblings.

Jesus calls Christian leaders to learn about people before making judgment. If a positive relationship occurs, then feelings of goodwill are in order. This passage relates to competitors, as well. Unfortunately, many business management writers teach that business is like war and you must fight against your competitors. However, if we follow Jesus' teaching here, we must approach competitors with feelings of goodwill and seek ways to collaborate instead of seeking destructive competitive methods.

This does not mean that we stop operating as separate companies. For instance, the Japanese taught United States firms how to work in symbiosis. Japanese firms shared research and exploration, and then each firm, using the jointly gained information, developed the best products possible for the customer.

There was a time when my printing company had a fire in the plant. It was a small fire with minimal damage, but it was big enough to get a mention on the 6:00 p.m. news. At 6:30 p.m. I received a call from a major competitor who had seen the news report, and to my surprise was calling to see if we needed additional press capacity. He offered to provide one of his presses for us to use while the damage was repaired. The competitor's action showed love and concern. We did not need the capacity since the fire did not affect any of the production equipment, but I can tell you that from that moment on, my attitude toward the competitor was one of support and concern Our two firms later worked together on joint ventures that benefited both of our firms, and especially our mutual customers. Would this have been possible had we hated each other? Of course not. Jesus calls us to think, feel, and behave in ways that bless everyone around us, including ourselves. This must start with our heart attitude. Matthew 12:34 says

> *"You brood of vipers, how can you who are evil say anything good? For out of the overflow of the heart the mouth speaks."*

And Matthew 15:18 says

> *"But the things that come out of the mouth come from the heart, and these make a man 'unclean.'"*

In this first verse, Jesus is responding to the Pharisees, and in the second verse, Jesus is explaining a parable to his disciples. Jesus' message throughout the New Testament continually stresses and re-stresses the spirit of God's original message.

Now, re-read this Sermon on the Mount passage and the one before it as a single passage showing the interpretation of the law and the spirit of the law. This passage is about heart-attitude, not pacifism. This concludes Jesus' teaching on the heart, and then he turns to observable behavior and the correct reasons for the behavior.

Lifestyle and Motive (Being Good Rather than Looking Good)

> *Matthew 6:1-4: "Be careful not to do your 'acts of righteousness' before men, to be seen by them. If you do, you will have no reward from your Father in heaven.*

So when you give to the needy, do not announce it with trumpets, as the hypocrites do in the synagogues and on the streets, to be honored by men. I tell you the truth, they have received their reward in full. But when you give to the needy, do not let your left hand know what your right hand is doing, so that your giving may be in secret. Then your Father, who sees what is done in secret, will reward you."

Augsburger (1982) addresses this section of the Sermon on the Mount as Jesus' treatment on lifestyle and motive. Jesus selected the three most important elements of Jewish religious tradition: almsgiving, prayer, and fasting and brought them to the forefront. I combine them because the message is the same in all three. Jesus condemns service with an ulterior motive and emphasizes service for the sake of righteousness. The New International Version of the Scriptures translates this into *"acts of righteousness,"* and the King James translates it into *"alms"* from the Greek word *eleemosune* meaning *"compassionateness, beneficence,"* or *"good deeds."* Jesus calls the *agapao* leader to behave in righteous ways because it is the right thing to do. This behavior is in contrast to the actions of a leader who participates in company functions just so that upper leadership might see him *"being"* good. These actions are also in contrast to the leader who would offer training to a younger leader as a way of proving what a good corporate citizen he is. Jesus says that God will not reward leaders who do acts with a hidden agenda, because the leaders have already received their rewards.

While we should behave in a private ways, we should also expect God to acknowledge us publicly. For a long time, I did not understand this passage and I interpreted the text to

117

mean that leaders should do good deeds out of the public's sight, so that if anyone found out and gave recognition, the act of kindness would be even more out in the open, thus further violating Jesus' teaching. But what the passage really says is to do acts of kindness with the right attitude of just wanting to help for the sake of wanting to help. If you receive recognition and gratitude from someone as a result, accept it warmly and sincerely, but never do the act expecting a reward.

I suppose the question is, "Do you want to serve or to be served?" Servant leadership teaches that we should follow Jesus' teaching to do good acts with the right motive. Think about yourself, or someone that you know, who agrees to speak before a group of people. After the event, when the participants are preparing to leave, the speaker lingers near the table or podium in hope that people will come and say how much they enjoyed the speech. Did the speaker come to serve or to be served? While everyone enjoys a compliment, Jesus warns us to be aware of our motives behind our behavior. Do you act because you thought you would get a compliment, or did you act because it was the right thing to do?

Treasures in Heaven (Building Righteous Relationships that You Can Take With You!)

Matthew 6:19-21 "Do not store up for yourselves treasures on earth, where moth and rust destroy, and where thieves break in and steal. But store up for yourselves treasures in heaven, where moth and rust do not destroy, and where thieves do not break in and steal. For where your treasure is, there your heart will be also."

Jesus follows the *"motive"* passage with a *"reward"* passage. There is a saying that *"money follows ministry"* and Jesus assures us that God honors our actions if we perform them for the sake of righteousness. In this particular passage, Jesus compares the rewards of this world with the rewards of heaven. He does not condemn possessing material goods; He condemns seeking them as the primary focus in life. Paul repeats this message later to Timothy in 1 Timothy 6:10

> *"For the love of money is the root of all evil: which while some coveted after, they have erred from the faith, and pierced themselves through with many sorrows."*

The passage from Matthew 6:19-21 builds upon the previous passages about motive in order to show that not only do you need the right motive, you need the right focus. Jesus also gives the Jewish community a measuring tool to use in judging others. He says, *"Where your treasure is so also is your heart."* People will be able to see the focus of your heart by the treasures that you store. The Greek word for *"heart"* is *kardia* that means *"the thoughts or feelings of a person."* Here we see a connection to the Beatitude of being pure in heart.

Leaders and supervisors usually have demands put upon them to perform toward specific goals and objectives that provide gain for their organizations. Companies that primarily seek to gain wealth will become known as being interested only in their customers' money. Supervisors that store up reports of high output at the expense of their employees' health and welfare will be known as the supervisor to be avoided. When the firm puts the customer ahead of profit they will be known to customers as a firm that can help them. And, the supervisor who puts the health

119

and welfare of employees first will be known by employees as the one to work for. Why wouldn't people want to work for leaders that look out for their employees' interests? This is a reciprocal relationship. The employer is looking out for the employee, hence, the employee is looking out for the employer.

Be Singled Minded (Keeping the Main Thing the Main Thing)

> *Matthew 6: 22-24 "The eye is the lamp of the body. If your eyes are good, your whole body will be full of light. But if your eyes are bad, your whole body will be full of darkness. If then the light within you is darkness, how great is that darkness!*
>
> *No one can serve two masters. Either he will hate the one and love the other, or he will be devoted to the one and despise the other. You cannot serve both God and money."*

This Scripture passage relates to the passage that we just covered and reveals that the central force of behavior behind the motive is integrity. The word *"lamp"* is the Greek word *luchnos* meaning *"a portable lamp"* or *"illuminator,"* perhaps a candle. The word *"light"* is the Greek word *photeinos* meaning *"lustrous"* or *"well illuminated."* The third use of *"light"* in this passage is the Greek word *phos* meaning *"luminescence in the widest form."* The New International Version translates this passage: *"If your eyes are good,"* while the King James is a more literal translation with, *"If your eye be single."* The Greek word *haplos* means *"to be single,"* which communicates focus in vision. Jesus uses a complex metaphor here speaking of eyes and light and body. If a person has clear eyesight, then his body can operate well. But if the eyes are cloudy with disease or damaged tissue, then the body does not receive the full picture of the surrounding world. Even more intense is the image of the blind person who is unable to receive any visual clues from the outside world. Jesus tells us that if we do not focus on what is good, our vision will be cloudy and dark.

Today, we often say that people are looking through "dark lenses," or "rose-colored glasses," or that someone "can see clearly." The analogies imply that the filters used to see the environment around us determine what we see. Our spiritual worldview is another expression that we use to filter what we gather through our eyes. Thus, to see things perfectly, we must have clear eyes that are devoid of all evil. Leaders may find themselves forming opinions about an employee's idea before actually hearing the presentation, all because the leader is blind to the truth. Leaders and supervisors must ensure that their eyes are clear and singularly focused. Once focused, all secondary things become clear.

Jesus continues with His thoughts on focus and single-mindedness by explaining that man cannot serve two masters. The Greek word *antechomai* means "to hold fast" or "to support," from which we translate "devoted," and the Greek word *kataphroneo* means to "think against" or "disesteem," from which we translate "despise." When Jesus used the word mammon, He may have referred to the Chaldean god of money or to "avarice." It is quite possible that He talks about both, and possibly even a third use of the term, "the deification of money." All three could be at play here, and it would have made an interesting word play during Jesus' lecture. Jesus' point is that you must serve one primary master, and that the Jewish community had to decide if it was going to serve God or if it was to focus on gaining earthly treasures. From the arrangement of the passages, it is quite possible that many in the audience were concentrating on gaining earthly treasures.

Do Not Worry (God is in Control – Reduce Your Stress Level)

> *Matthew 6:25-34: "Therefore I tell you, do not worry about your life, what you will eat or drink; or about your body, what you will wear. Is not life more important than food, and the body more important than clothes? Look at the birds of the air; they do not sow or reap or store away in barns, and yet your heavenly Father feeds them. Are you not much more valuable than they? Who of you by worrying can add a single hour to his life?*
>
> *And why do you worry about clothes? See how the lilies of the field grow. They do not labor or spin. Yet I tell you that not even Solomon in all his splendor was dressed like one of these. If that is how God clothes the grass of the field, which is here today and tomorrow is thrown into the fire, will he not much more clothe you, O you of little faith? So do not worry, saying, 'What shall we eat?' or 'What shall we drink?' or 'What shall we wear?' For the pagans run after all these things, and your heavenly Father knows that you need them. But seek first his kingdom and his righteousness, and all these things will be given to you as well. Therefore do not worry about tomorrow, for tomorrow will worry about itself. Each day has enough trouble of its own."*

How surprising it must have been for those people to hear Jesus instruct listeners to not worry about their lives. Life was especially hard during Bible times. The Greek word used for *"worry"* is *merimnao* and it means, *"to be anxious about."* Today, many people express fear in the workplace, not fear of a fellow co-worker doing physical harm to them, but fear of what will happen if they fail. Workers usually fear that they will lose their jobs if they do not do what their supervisor wants. I have talked to hundreds of people who, out of fear, did things on the job that they knew were not ethical totally out of fear. This passage is especially for those employees. Remember the story in the Beatitude of Peacemaking about writing the letter of resignation and leaving the date blank? Well, it applies here too.

Jesus calls us to seek first the kingdom. *"Seek"* in Greek is the word *zeteo* that means to *"require"* or *"to seek after."* *"Added"* comes from the Greek word *prostithemi* meaning, *"add,"* *"increase,"* or *"proceed further."* Jesus is continuing a message that He presented earlier by saying that having material items is all right as long as it is not your main focus. He emphasizes that God will provide for your wants if you operate in righteous ways. The paradox of the Christian lifestyle is that we get the material things that we do not seek, when we first seek righteousness. Leaders should seek what is right for the company and not just the next promotion. Leaders should seek what is right for the employees and not for the extra ounce of production they can get out of them. Companies should promote the leaders who seek what is right because companies want what is best for the firm. Employees will produce the *"extra ounce"* of production simply because they find joy in serving a righteous supervisor.

I once heard that a politician acts in ways that benefit his next election while a statesman acts in ways that helps the next generation. I think Jesus calls us to be statesmen and to do what is right for the organization rather than what is right for us individually.

If we stop worrying about tomorrow and live righteously today, tomorrow will take care of itself (with God's help, of course). And whom would you rather have in control of tomorrow – God or you?

Judging Others (Be Willing to Submit to the Same Criteria by Which You Judge)

> *Matthew 7:1-6: "Do not judge, or you too will be judged. For in the same way you judge others, you will be judged, and with the measure you use, it will be measured to you.*
>
> *Why do you look at the speck of sawdust in your brother's eye and pay no attention to the plank in your own eye? How can you say to your brother, 'Let me take the speck out of your eye,' when all the time there is a plank in your own eye? You hypocrite, first take the plank out of your own eye, and then you will see clearly to remove the speck from your brother's eye.*
>
> *Do not give dogs what is sacred; do not throw your pearls to pigs. If you do, they may trample them under their feet, and then turn and tear you to pieces."*

Many Christians read this passage and believe that we are never to judge anyone. This is not the case, for in many other places, Scripture asks us to judge. Scripture calls us to test (meaning to judge) the spirits of a man and see if what he teaches is true. We judge not by the outward appearance, but by the inward appearance of the man. The first verses of this passage are simply the Law of Reciprocity in action. Jesus explains to the Jewish community that whatever standard of worth they use to measure another, they should be willing to be measured by themselves. Writers on this subject (Augsburger, Eddleman, and Govett) believe that Jesus tells us not to judge at all. But in reality, there are times to judge and times not to judge. The following Scriptures give credence to the belief that we should judge: Leviticus 19:5; 27:12; Numbers 35:24; Deuteronomy 1:16; 16:18; 17:12: 1 Samuel 3:13; Proverbs 20:8; 31:9; John 8:15; Acts 4:19; 1 Corinthians 5:12; 6:6; 10:15; and 11:13. Equally important, there are also passages in Scripture that tell us God should be the only judge of certain actions. It is important that we know when and how to judge and be willing to submit to the same criteria.

Emmet Fox (1966) said it clearly, "[t]he plain fact is that it is the Law of Life that, as we think, and speak, and act towards others, so will others think, and speak, and act towards us." Leaders who evaluate employees in the dreaded annual employee evaluation should consider whether they would want superiors evaluating them by the same criteria.

Over the past years, I have written several documents for use in my courses. Students know that my writing contains considerable typos and grammatical mistakes. I tell students that while I will grade them on their use of English and grammar, they should grade me by the same criteria when it is time for the course evaluation. It is hard to accept this criticism. Sometimes I feel that I would like to criticize their work, but not allow them to criticize mine. However, I know that as I judge them, I must willingly accept their judgment based on the same criteria.

Remember Jesus' teaching in an earlier passage about not hating your enemy just because he or she is different? Jesus is reinforcing this concept in this passage. How often do people judge another because of the color of their skin, the appearance of their clothes, or their speech dialect? If you judge people in any of these ways, you must be willing for them to judge you on the same criteria. Earlier, I mentioned that I grew up in a small rural farming community in the Midwest. There were no African-American families in this little community of 2,000 residents. One day, an African-American family moved to town and rented a trailer in the local trailer park. The family had two children; one of them was a boy my age that was in my class at school. During his first week, I socialized with the boy during lunch and recess and enjoyed his company. But then he told me that his family was moving away. I asked why but he wouldn't say. I learned some time later that the town leaders forced the family to leave because of the color of their skin. I never understood why and still do not understand. I would hope that we could judge people by their hearts rather than their skin. The Book of Acts provides an excellent example of how to judge correctly. After Paul's conversion and training, the Christians still did not trust him and judged him to be evil until Paul proved his transformation to them. When the Christian leaders saw Paul's heart and understood Paul's new birth, the leaders judged him to be good and welcomed him into their lives. Can you imagine what would have happened if Christians had judged Paul solely on his past without consideration for his conversion? Jesus couched this whole discussion this way, before you are going to pick on something small and petty in a person's life, you had better consider the big awful thing in your own life. That is what Jesus meant in his analogy of the speck and the mote. No one is perfect, and no one has the right to judge someone acting as if they themselves are perfect. If we are going to judge at all, it needs to be from the perspective of knowing that we also have defects that others should point out in order for us to improve.

Proverbs 27:17 tells us that one man sharpens another just as iron sharpens iron. Each man challenges the other to improve and by this process, each person becomes better. But, if only one person is judging and the other is constantly submitting, then there can only be limited improvement.

Leaders should take heed of this concept and seek as much judgment from employees as they mete out in judgment to employees. With leaders and followers challenging each other, both can improve. This is, of course, totally contrary to much of the leadership in the United States today. We see many leaders prowling around the office roaring judgments like angry lions. Here's the truth, real lions do not need to roar, they just need to be lions, and respect will follow.

I hear many employees complain that the leader who judges them is not competent to do the employee's job. I have seen this to be true in many cases and wonder how a leader might accurately judge the work of another if he is incapable of doing the job. Is the leader willing to let someone who cannot do his job judge him? Does he or she have a choice? If someone who cannot do his job judges the leader, how credible can the evaluation be? In the final verse of this passage, we are introduced to the recognizable concept of "casting pearls before swine." What Jesus is telling us is to have discernment in our judgment. If we find someone who is unworthy to receive valuable things, don't reward them, hence, don't cast pearls before swine, for whatever reason. The Jewish audience to whom Jesus spoke did not have much use for pigs, at all (although there was a sect of the Hebrews in the area that raised and ate pork). This is a difficult passage to apply to leaders and supervisors because of the obvious reference in Scripture to what is sacred, but let's see what happens when we look closer. Many leaders and supervisors practice *"closed-mouth"* leadership styles in contrast to *"open-book"* leadership. First there is the belief that too much information entrusted to employees will prove harmful to the company in some way. But there is another way of looking at this. If company information is a matter of record, there should be nothing in the records that can ultimately hurt the company. If you judge the employee to be good in heart, then share the information. If you judge the employee to be bad in heart, then do not give information. The good employee is interested in the firm's goodwill, and the bad employee is interested in his or her own goodwill. The leader must judge with discernment.

Ask, Seek, and Knock (Persevere and Serve)

> *Matthew 7:7-12: "Ask and it will be given to you; seek and you will find; knock and the door will be opened to you. For everyone who asks receives; he who seeks finds; and to him who knocks, the door will be opened.*
>
> *Which of you, if his son asks for bread, will give him a stone? Or if he asks for a fish, will give him a snake? If you, then, though you are evil, know how to give good gifts to your children, how much more will your Father in heaven give good gifts to those who ask him! So in everything, do to others what you would have them do to you, for this sums up the Law and the Prophets."*

In these verses, the Greek words for *"ask," "seek,"* and *"knock,"* imply a continual state of activity. These words could actually read, *"Ask and keep on asking, seek and keep on seeking, knock and keep on knocking."* Jesus encourages His followers to keep continuously petitioning God for what they need. Jesus is reminding the Jewish community there on the hillside that even they, as mere humans, treat their children well and such it is with their Heavenly Father who desires, all the more, to treat His children well.

Eddleman (1957) reminds us that this passage supports the earlier passages on judgment, discernment, and action. He illustrates this by showing that if a child asks for bread, the father would not give a stone (people of this period baked bread in a flat hard form that someone might mistake for a stone if given only an undiscriminating look).

I think that this passage goes much deeper for leaders and supervisors concerning behavior toward employees. Consider the employee who asks for new tools to perform her work because the current tools are insufficient. The leader should examine the facts, test the heart of the employee, and if at all possible, give her the tools. So often I observe leaders and supervisors who take employees' requests and cut the actual request in half just on general principle. Do I need to remind you of the reciprocal component to this act? Will the employee be motivated to give her best effort? Sometimes leaders and supervisors set production objectives artificially high just to test the employees. This is generally unproductive and can generate mistrust between employees and their leaders.

Another effect that can occur is that employees soon learn their managers' "tricks" and begin to ask for more than what's actually needed to try to ensure that they will have what they need. These reactions are not surprising. Leaders should give employees what they need to do their work, presuming that there are sufficient funds to provide the equipment, and sufficient training as well as sufficient understanding of processes and methods to maximize the investment. In these situations, leaders are in the role of the "father" giving their "child," the employee, the bread or fish they need. Note that bread and fish were staple items of the diet during Jesus' time. Try interpreting this passage in light of staples in today's office setting.

If leaders do not want employees padding budgets and cutting back on targets, then leaders should give employees what they need. Leaders find themselves in the "employee" role when they must ask for budgets and targets from those above them. How much better would it be if we all asked for what we really needed and produced what could really accomplish, without playing the "fake negotiating game."

A Tree and Its Fruit (Task Completion is Central to Leadership Activity)

> *Matthew 7:16-20: "Watch out for false prophets. They come to you in sheep's clothing, but inwardly they are ferocious wolves. By their fruit you will recognize them. Do people pick grapes from thorn bushes, or figs from thistles? Likewise every good tree bears good fruit, but a bad tree bears bad fruit. A good tree cannot bear bad fruit, and a bad tree cannot bear good fruit. Every tree that does not bear good fruit is cut down and thrown into the fire. Thus, by their fruit you will recognize them."*

This passage is a major continuation of Jesus' theme. He stated earlier that people will speak and behave in ways that are consistent with their hearts or values. Here, He admonishes the audience to observe what others do and to judge the results. He is expanding his thought now by warning about people who might temporarily alter their appearance or actions to mislead others.

Jesus advises us to watch for the long-term results of an individual's efforts, explaining that by this you will know the true person. He tells us that as we observe people's values in action we can tell what kind of fruit they willyield. Sometimes fruit takes a long time to grow, and the appearance of buds and flowers, and even the earliest sign of fruit are not true indications of what the ultimate fruit will look like. In fact, Jesus is training us to become trained observers of people; you might even say "people-fruit examiners."

Many times we interview people and hire them because they appear to be very competent and just what we want and need in a particular job opening. Only later we discover that the person is not as good as we thought. Leaders and supervisors should evaluate people in the workplace for some time before they allow people to have significant responsibility. This requires us as leaders to allow workers to go through the various stages of growth: pollination, blossoming, and bearing fruit. We must fertilize and add water if we want to be able to see what kind of fruit we can expect in a person's life. This passage also emphasizes the works of the person as proof of the heart. So often we have a tendency to look at either a person's heart or their accomplishments when we actually need to observe both.

Earl Palmer (1986) uses this passage to demonstrate the ethical concept of "ends vs. means." Palmer believes that Jesus does not see ethical behavior as merely ends or merely means, but rather a combination of the two. Thus, we moved toward situational ethics. This is difficult for most people to accept since it places the ethical decision in the hands of each person to do as they wish. On the other hand, this may not be difficult to accept if we live by the rules Jesus taught in this Sermon.

The Wise and Foolish Builders (If You Know Something is True – Live By It!)

> *Matthew 7:24-28: "Therefore everyone who hears these words of mine and puts them into practice is like a wise man who built his house on the rock. The rain came down, the streams rose, and the winds blew and beat against that house; yet it did not fall, because it had its foundation on the rock. But everyone who hears these words of mine and does not put them into practice is like a foolish man who built his house on sand. The rain came down, the streams rose, and the winds blew and beat against that house, and it fell with a great crash."*

Jesus concludes His teaching with a wonderful analogy that summarizes the importance of His points. The Greek word for "put them into practice" is *poleo* that implies "a wide application without delay." To make our application clear, Jesus uses the analogy of a home with a firm foundation to demonstrate how we as leaders need to build our lives upon Him. The wise leader and supervisor will listen to lessons Jesus taught from the mountainside and put them into action immediately.

Selah

How do you measure up to the standards that are presented in the second half of the Sermon on the Mount? I, for one, know I have a long way to go.

Take some time now before you go on in this book, and review the sections in this chapter. Now write a few notes to yourself – either in this book or in a private journal, and note what areas you need to work on.

Then, hold a meeting with the staff that report directly to you (or with your peers in the organization if no one reports directly to you), and ask that they help you conform to this ideal that Jesus presented and ask that they help hold you accountable to the changes you need to make in your life. I found that some of my staff members were the best leadership trainers around. They have a lot at stake in your leadership!

Chapter 11: Harvesting the Fruit of *Agapao* Leadership

My purpose for this chapter is to show you how the Fruit of the Spirit can help you measure how much a leader lives by spiritual principles. At the risk of offending some traditional Bible scholars in this essay, I will take a different path of Scripture interpretation.

First, let me say that there is precious little material to help the common man or woman understand the Fruit of the Spirit passages found in chapter five of Paul's letter to the Galatians. I have found several books that attempt to show how the fruit results from accepting Christ, and I have found a few books written for the professional Bible scholar that provide little to no practical application of Scripture.

The one exception to this dearth of research is Bert Ghezzi's 1987 book, *Becoming More Like Jesus: Growth in the Spirit.* Therefore, much of what you find in this essay is my own understanding of the fifth chapter of Paul's letter to the Galatians.

Let us first examine the purpose of this passage. Why does Paul take time to write about these things? The church at Galatia was undergoing a difficult period during which many Jewish Christians believed that Old Testament laws were binding on the New Testament Church. As a result of much in-fighting, the church (some say many churches) faced radical division among its members. Paul learned that it was more than just legal interpretation that had infected the church. People who had accepted Jesus as the Messiah and who had started to live by His teaching were falling away from the spiritual principles and were returning to a sinful nature.

134

In the Sermon on the Mount (Matthew 5), Jesus taught the Jewish community that if they lived according to the principles laid down by God; there would be little need for man to make laws and regulations. At the beginning of Galatians Chapter Five, Paul is instructing the members of the churches about this same topic. Paul reminds the church that it is free, in Christ, to live peacefully, and he admonishes them for not living a life according to spiritual principles. To illustrate the difference between the way the church members live and how they ought to live, Paul describes both.

In Galatians 5:19, Paul describes the characteristics of a life grounded in a sinful nature. He mentions sexual immorality, impurity and debauchery, idolatry and witchcraft, hatred, discord, jealousy, fits of rage, selfish ambition, dissension, factions and envy, drunkenness, and orgies and the like.

He then describes the characteristics of the spiritually principled life based on love, joy, peace, patience, kindness, goodness, faithfulness, gentleness, and self-control—or the Fruits of the Spirit.

These characteristics are the result of a life lived according to spiritual principles, not a result of labor or works. These characteristics, or qualities, parallel The Beatitudes found in Matthew 5. The Beatitudes describe the inward traits and principles that a godly person possesses. The Fruit of the Spirit represent the measurable outward manifestation of living a life led by spiritual principles.

Much debate has ensued over the past several centuries as to what Paul meant by the Fruit of the Spirit. Some say that "fruit" is a singular word and, therefore, all the terms that follow are simply different ways to describe love. Others say that *"fruit"* is also plural, and, therefore, the terms describe different aspects of a fervent spiritual life.

A simple look at the Greek in this passage does not support a restrictive interpretation. Rather, the passage is quite simple, and yet very powerful. Paul contrasts the outward characteristics of a life following a sinful nature with a life following a spiritual nature. Paul says nothing that we could interpret about restricting a life based on spiritual principles to only those who follow Jesus. Some writers claim that Christian virtue comes only from the Holy Spirit. Paul does not say that in this passage. He does say that living out the sinful nature is contrary to living by the Spirit. The Greek word that we translate as *"spirit"* is *pneuma*, which means *"ghost, life, spirit, angel, and/or divine spirit." Pneuma* occurs throughout the New Testament when referring to spirit.

Let's dig deeper beginning with the word fruit since it seems to cause so much trouble for some people. The Greek word *karpos* implies a literal or figurative fruit that someone plucks from a tree or plant. This word implies a fruit deliberately harvested in contrast to a fruit that is not domesticated or sought by someone. The Greek word implies both the single and plural form just as the English word fruit could mean a basket of golden apples, mixed apples, or mixed fruit. We in the United States think of apples as fruit. In Paul's time, and in the area of Asia Minor where the Galatian churches existed, the grape or fig would be a better symbol for fruit. The word implies something that is the result of growth and care that eventually results in a harvest.

A good harvest occurs because the grower follows the principles of good agriculture and because God provides timely rains and appropriate environmental conditions for excellent growth. Nothing grows because of the law. Regarding Paul's fruit analogy, let's think of the fruit as a bunch of grapes for a moment. The grapes provide evidence of the type of vine that is supporting their growth. The appearance and quality of the grapes may even give evidence of the vine grower and the vineyard.

Fruit is the result of process. Grapes, for example, do not just appear one day on a vine. They must first be planted, then they must be provided with proper nutrients, and given the right environment in which to grow. But once this is done, the fruit just naturally grows. Still, there is more process. The grapes form as buds and then develop into fruit. Likewise, when we walk in the Spirit, we are compelled to do as the Spirit would do, not because we force ourselves through good works to bear good fruit, but because it comes naturally through the Spirit. When we live according to scriptural principles we will produce good fruit. It's not us alone, though; it's through Him. The fruit is His characteristic, not our own. We produce good fruit as a result of the Vine to which we are attached, and because our Vine provides us with wonderful nutrients, not to mention life itself.

The Clustering of the Fruit of the Spirit

Scripture is fascinating in that there are so many relationships and groupings of ideas and concepts. The Fruit of the Spirit are clustered in groups of three. The first cluster of three includes: (1) love, (2) joy, and (3) peace. The second cluster includes: (4) patience, (5) kindness, and (6) goodness. The third cluster includes: (7) faithfulness, (8) gentleness, and (9) self-control. Of further interest is the relationship of each group to the whole. The first group represents a macro aspect of relationship and behavior. One might say that it represents the fruit of man relating to God. The second group represents a mid-range concept of how man might relate to society or other groups of people. The last set of three fruits represents a micro view of the fruit that develops when one relates to another using scriptural principles. Although there is little written on this subject, I encourage you to consider these clusters of fruit as they hang on the Vine of life. Consider the fruit as an element of its group as you work through each of the following nine fruits.

Love (Man relating to God)

We should examine each fruit in sequence to fully understand its significance. The first is love. Love, as used here, comes from the Greek word *agape*, which is the strongest of the four Greek words that translate into love. Each of the individual meanings for the word love includes: *eros*, *philos*, *agapao*, and *agape*. Jesus used the term *agape* when He referred to God's love for us. The first type of love that is mentioned in the Fruits of the Spirit is *Agape* love, a self-sacrificing love characterized by one giving of oneself so that another may be blessed. The giver expects nothing in return or as a result of the behavior. This is God-like love for us and it makes it easier to understand how the word *Agape* also translates into "a love feast." A love feast is exactly the type of love that God wants to experience with us. Don't let modern images rush to your mind, we are talking about an abundance of pure, undefiled, selfless love streaming from the cross of Calvary to us today.

Joy (Man relating to God)

Paul lists joy as the second characteristic of living by spiritual principles. The Greek word that we translate into "joy" is *chara*, which encompasses "exceeding joy," "cheerfulness," and "calm." Paul used the same word in Romans 14:17; 15:13, 32; and Philippians 1:4, 25. There are over 50 references to *chara* in the New Testament. Other translations of joy come from the Greek words *agalliasis* and *euphrosune* meaning "gladness."

Joy is the second of the three macro-fruits referring to the leader's relationship with God. The fruit, though, is also demonstrated in the leader's outward behavior toward people in the workplace. Man's relationship with God is often mirrored in his behavior toward others.

When a leader lives by spiritual principles there is always a sense of calmness about him or her. When stress and pressure surround the workplace, employees always gravitate to the leader who lives by the Spirit, for in that leader there is a sense of calm. The leader who lives by spiritual principles exhibits cheerfulness in all situations and has a kind word for any occasion.

When difficult projects begin to weigh heavily on the minds of employees, the leader's first reaction should be to bring a sense of calm and lightness to the workplace. I remember a time when my company bought a competing company. During the transition period, there was a great deal of stress in the new subsidiary. I remember one of the leaders who stayed on after the purchase asking me when I thought the transition time would be over. I told him he would know it when he heard laughter in the pressroom. He nodded and commented that there had not been a sense of joy in the workplace for many years. Six weeks later, the same leader walked by my office and stopped to tell me that he had just heard pressmen laughing. He noticed that they all were going about their work cheerfully. The leader smiled, said "Thanks," and continued on with his work.

Dr. William Edwards Deming, in his book, *The New Economics,* taught countless companies in post WWII that living by his 14 principles would result in joy in the workplace. Deming, a strong Christian, used Scripture at selected times to support his concepts. I believe that Deming considered the Greek word *chara* when he said workers would experience *"joy."*

Joy does not always mean hilarity. There is a sense of control in a workplace that has a spiritually led leader. By joy, one might envision people waking up in the morning with a sense of happiness and a positive expectation of what will happen at work that day. As I begin to understand more of the spiritual principles and attempt to live by them, I notice the changes in my workplace and in the people I manage. On several instances, I have found employees coming to work on their days off or on vacation days. When I asked them why they have come to the office, each answered in a like manner, *"I wanted to get this project finished. Besides, I enjoy being here."* Joy is a communicable condition. It literally infects those around you. This characteristic is closely aligned with the next characteristic – peace. This fruit is one of the three macro fruits that deal with a relationship with God. When a leader enjoys a strong relationship with God, there is an outgrowth of joy and happiness to all others in the workplace.

Peace (Man relating to God)

Paul uses the Greek word *eirene* here, and again in 2 Timothy 2:22, to imply *"quietness"* and *"rest."* We find *"peace"* used 88 times in the New Testament. Eighty-six of these occurrences are the word *eirene.* Other words that the King James Bible uses for the word peace are *sigao* and *hesuchazo,* which mean, *"to hold silent"* or *"keep peace."*

One of the principles described by Jesus in The Beatitudes is "Blessed are the peacemakers." Paul's use of *eirene* follows Jesus' teaching that peace is the result of other behaviors and activities. Peace must be created and sustained. It is noteworthy that in The Beatitudes the word for peacemaker is *eirenopoios*, meaning, "to do peace." Paul uses the noun form of the same word that Jesus used as a verb.

Eirene builds upon the concept of calm found in the *chara*. It is interesting to see how the Fruits of the Spirit build upon each other. Since peace is the last of the macro cluster illustrating the leader's relationship with God, it is interesting to see how having peace with God develops into a relationship with people. Employees seek to work for leaders when peace abounds in the workplace. I interviewed a senior leader at the Christian Broadcasting Network (CBN) who, I believed, exemplified this concept of peace. He had worked for CBN longer than most and seemed to survive a lot of the ups and downs that a major organization undergoes. As a part of my interviewing process, I talked with people who worked for this leader and with others who knew people who had worked for him. I felt that if I went beyond the first circle of employees, I would better understand him. What I found was that a sense of peace surrounded all of this leader's activities. His employees demonstrated the lowest turnover in the organization. There was even a list of people who wanted to work for him. Everyone agreed that more work was accomplished in his department than in most others, yet there was little evidence of stress or of overburdened work conditions. His department was busy, but peaceful. Employees told me that they felt more rested after a day's work than when they began. Some described what he did as miraculous; I described it as *eirene*.

Employees can easily spot leaders who live by spiritual principles. These leaders are the people that others turn to in times of strife and trouble, or to learn the truth about the organization. These leaders bring about a sense of order amid the chaos of organizational change. It is only out of peace that one can have patience.

Patience (Man relating to others in society)

Paul uses the Greek word *makrothamiz* to refer to our word "patience." The King James translation uses the word long-suffering, which we might translate today into "forbearance." Another definition that we could use is "fortitude." Paul also uses *makrothamiz* in 2 Timothy 3:10 and Colossians 3:12. Paul also used the word *makrothamiz* in Romans 2:4, 9:22; 2 Corinthians 6:6; and Ephesians 4:2. It's important to not assign a "poor me" attitude to the word patience, perhaps because of the King James "long suffering" inference. But there is nothing "poor me" about living a life according to spiritual principles.

I encourage you to consider the combined definitions of fortitude and patience. You can recognize leaders who live by spiritual principles because they understand the concept of time and seasons. There is a time to plant, to tend, to wait, and to harvest. Isaiah understood this characteristic when he wrote, "but those who wait on the Lord will renew their strength. They will soar on wings like eagles; they will run and not grow weary, they will walk and not be faint" (40:31). Isaiah used the Hebrew word *qavah*, meaning "to wait patiently" or "to look patiently." I believe that we can tie this to the Greek word *kairos* meaning "the opportune time." Patience is an observable characteristic of waiting for the right time to act and never rushing an event or person.

Leaders who live by spiritual principles demonstrate patience when working with employees. This fruit, patience, is the first fruit that deals with our relationships with other people. Patience is not an all-encompassing acceptance of what employees do, but rather it's an understanding that all people learn and develop at different rates of speed. Leaders also know that after a new program is inaugurated, it needs time to grow without constant intervention. Many times, employees describe leaders who exhibit patience as "caring about people." While these leaders certainly care for people, it is probably even more accurate that the leader is simply patient with employees. Another word that employees use to describe patient leaders is gentle.

H. Auden wrote in his 1962 poem, *The Dyer's Hand*:

> *Perhaps there is only one cardinal sin: impatience. Because of impatience we were driven out of Paradise, because of impatience we cannot return." Patience is the result of understanding the "when" as well as the "how."*

When I think of this fruit, I see leaders who <u>do not</u> live by spiritual principles pushing people to make sales too early, to ship products too soon, or to try to perform new tasks before completing all the necessary training. I see the Challenger shuttle disaster. I see product recalls that could have been avoided. I see the Ford Pinto. I see airline leaders pushing pilots and locomotive engineers operating their equipment without enough rest. I see accidents that could have been avoided. Evidence of this fruit is reflected in having patience to see that everything is as it should be.

Gentleness (Man relating to others in society)

Paul continues the descriptive passage with the Greek word *chrestotes*. We translate *chrestotes* as "being kind or excellent in character." Jesus described just such a person in the Samaritan who helped the injured traveler after the thieves robbed him and the priests ignored him. The only other word found in the New Testament that we translate, as "gentleness" is the Greek word *epielkela*, meaning "mildness."

Leaders who live by spiritual principles might exhibit behaviors that others would describe as kindness, gentleness, or being excellent in character. A leader might demonstrate this characteristic by finding a job in the organization for an employee who had difficulty performing their assigned duties. Rather than firing the employee, the leader might seek a job commensurate with the employee's skills.

If it was necessary to terminate an employee, a leader who lived by spiritual principles might seek a way to ease the employee out of the workplace rather than fire the person in front of others. Unfortunately, gentleness is not a characteristic that many of today's organizations think leaders should possess. A recent book on the subject of "bosses from hell" described a leader who enjoyed firing people. This leader would tape a picture of the fired employee on the employee's chair and make rude remarks to the picture for several days after the termination.

A leader might exhibit gentleness by easing change into an organization. Ansoff described a concept called the "Accordion Method" of change whereby leaders introduced incremental measures of change and allowed employees to adjust to the change before introducing more. Employees could easily describe this type of leader as being gentle and good.

Goodness (Man relating to others in society)

The Greek word *agathosune*, used here for goodness, also translates into *"virtue"* or *"beneficence." The American Heritage Dictionary* defines beneficence as *"the state or quality of being kind, charitable, or beneficial."*

The concept of goodness found in the Greek word brings with it an understanding that the goodness must be good for something. There are only four occasions where we see *agathosune* used in the New Testament: Romans 15:14; Galatians 5:22; Ephesians 5:9; and 2 Thessalonians 1:11.

Leaders might exhibit this fruit by showing more interest in the well being of employees rather than in the bottom line. This is not to say that there is no concern for fiscal responsibility, but rather that leaders living by spiritual principles must value people above money. This definition includes the word beneficial. This implies that a leader's actions, while charitable to the employee(s), also must be for the greatest good of all. Looking at goodness and patience, we can see many similarities, thus supporting the logic of the group of three fruits that all center on how we treat each other as humans. Gentleness can also be viewed as goodness. Gentleness can become a form of charitable behavior when the well being of others becomes a higher priority than self. Leaders could exhibit this fruit by sharing information with employees. So often we see leaders who keep the truth about change from employees. The sudden introduction of change occurs as leaders try to effect organizational change before employees have a chance to argue or sabotage the works. Yet, if leaders showed the employees the benefits of change and helped reluctant employees make the transition, the organization would be better off in the long run. I think many leaders do not do this because they either do not understand the change, they do not care about the well being of the employees, or they don't know enough to realize that there is a better way to operate.

Faithfulness (A leader relating to another individual)

The next fruit in this sequence is faithfulness, translated from the Greek word *pistis*, which means, *"assurance, belief, fidelity, and constancy."* Paul also uses this term in 1 Timothy 6:11 and 2 Timothy 2:22. *Pistis* occurs 237 times in the New Testament. Only nine times do we translate the word faith from other Greek words. Among these few exceptions, the most notable would be the Greek word *oligopistos*, which means *"lacking confidence or faith."* Faithfulness introduces us to the last group of three fruits. Leaders exhibit this fruit in many ways. To begin with, they are dependable. Employees and superiors both know that they can trust leaders who operate by spiritual principles to complete a task. Employees and superiors know that these leaders stay for the long haul. W. E. Deming included *"too much mobility of leadership"* as one of his seven deadly sins for United States leaders. Deming believed that there is too little loyalty among leaders toward their firms. Leaders who live by spiritual principles stay with a firm until God calls them to leave. This allows the firm to grow for the long-term. Consider the importance of faithfulness in the mentoring relationship between the leader and the employee.

Leaders who live by spiritual principles are trustworthy. You would not expect to find a spiritually principled leader arrested for embezzlement or insider trading. Employees feel confident that they can talk to a spiritually principled leader and not have personal information revealed to others.

Leaders exhibit this fruit by showing belief in employees. Leaders following spiritual principles know when employees are ready for more responsibility and encourage employees to excel in the new areas. There is a sense of encouragement and equipping that pervades a firm led by spiritually principled leaders.

Meekness (A leader relating to another individual)

Paul uses the Greek word *praotes*, which comes from the root word praus implying controlled discipline as we saw in The Beatitudes. *Praotes* also translates as *"gentleness."* We again see the circular entwining of the essence of the fruits. Leaders exhibit this fruit by controlling their organizational strength and using only what is necessary to accomplish the task. No one would accuse a spiritually principled leader of *"throwing his or her weight around."*

Employees would see examples of meekness in the leader during times of correction and rebuke. The meek leader corrects employees when necessary, but does so in a way that causes the employee to grow. Unprincipled leaders correct people in hurtful ways that leave emotional scars on the employee.

Other employees can recognize the meek leader by how the leader works with other departments. The meek leader does not threaten or demand, but rather negotiates for cooperation in a way that builds goodwill and seeks peace in the organization.

Temperance or Self-control (A leader relating to another individual)

The last fruit is temperance, also called "self-control." From the Greek word, *egkrateia*, we translate "self-control" or "temperance." *Egkrateia* comes from the root word *egkrates* meaning "self-controlled in appetite" or "being temperate." I see this character in a leader who exhibits self-control in actions and words. This ties well into the idea of meekness being controlled discipline.

Leaders exhibiting this fruit would not seek to hoard resources or spend unnecessarily at the end of a budget cycle just to ensure money in the budget for the next cycle, but rather would seek to use resources for the greatest good of the organization. I believe leaders would exhibit this characteristic by being controlled in their personal lives, controlling the amount they eat and drink, and the amount of time spent in any one activity. Thus, a self-controlled leader is balanced in their approach to life.

Employees see the spiritually-principled leader as balanced and as someone whom they should emulate, often using the leader as an ideal to which they should emulate. Spiritually-principled leaders become the person from whom others seek advice and who demonstrate balance in their own lives.

Selah

How's your harvest going so far? Need some pruning? Or maybe some watering and care from the Vinedresser?

If you are not satisfied with your "fruit" harvest, go back to the chapter on The Beatitudes and the chapter on the second half of the Sermon on the Mount and see if you can find where you need to adopt or strengthen the values. Remember that the fruit are the result of living the life according to the Spirit (as defined in the Sermon on the Mount) and should not be sought as fruit alone. Rather, it is best if you look at the soil, the fertilizer, the water, the sun, the temperature, etc., and adjust as necessary so the right fruit will develop.

Chapter 12: Leadership According to Proverbs 31

As a leader, would you like to move above the level of mediocrity and stretch toward perfection in your work life? If so, this chapter is must reading for you. In it you will find advice from a collection of 22 verses that tell you how to behave and how to work so you might move closer to perfection as a leader.

Introduction to the Passage

Proverbs 31:10-32 contains 22 verses, each beginning in the Hebrew with a successive letter in the Hebrew alphabet (an acrostic). Although Cohen (1946) ascribes the author's name, Lemuel as a code name for Solomon, translating Lemuel as meaning: *"towards God,"* most writers, including Gibson (1986), Farmer (1991), and Ironside (1908) believe that the writer was a king named Lemuel.

Verses 10 through 32 are words of advice from the mother of a king, or perhaps a young prince, who is looking for a wife. Throughout the Book of Proverbs we see authors talking about the dangers of evil women. This passage of Proverbs is refreshing in its positive approach to women. Its placement in the passage is important since Hebrew teachings always ended with an important lesson.

Cohen (1946) points out that these 22 verses were recited from memory in the Jewish home on the Sabbath eve, thus setting a high standard for the Jewish wife and the young women of the household who aspired to attain this level of perfection. It also set a standard for the young men of the household who received constant instruction about the type of wife they were to seek. Now let me show you how this has bearing on the workplace. Consider the impact on United

States organizations if the human resource departments, all leaders, and all hiring supervisors, repeated the qualities of a perfect leader for the firm once each week. Would we not strive to live up to these high ideals and strive to hire new leaders that fit our concept of perfection?

Although the acrostic form of writing makes it easier to memorize the verses, it causes a literary problem of message construction because the first letter of the first word of each verse must fit the acrostic structure. Thus, we find the author of these 22 verses skipping from subject to subject. I encourage you to read the whole of Proverbs 31:10-21 and then focus on how the messages are grouped into the following categories: (a) an introduction to the passage; (b) relation to the workplace; (c) relation to self in the workplace; (d) relation to employees in the workplace; (e) relation to superiors in the workplace; and (f) relation to rewards in the workplace.

In case you're wondering, here's why you should study a passage on the ideal wife to understand the perfect leader. Several authors on Proverbs refer to the wife as a leader and a caretaker of the home (Toy, 1904; Aitken, 1986; & Cohen, 1946). Rylaarsdam (1964) adds to this understanding by pointing out that the wife, like many leaders, did not have ownership rights in the household, thus her labors could not increase her wealth. If you want a solid definition of a hard working overseer, this is what you're looking for. I think you'll be pleasantly surprised at the clear and powerful correlations.

Proverbs 31:10, "A wife of noble character who can find? She is worth far more than rubies."

The first verse of this passage implies that the senior leader of the organization recognizes that a leader of virtue and skill is invaluable. Note that virtue, from the Hebrew word *chayil,* has a broader depiction than just being morally righteous. The word also refers to ability, efficiency, and wealth (Hamel, 1992). It is rare to find a leader who not only has integrity, but also has the skills to perform the job, and a track record of efficient leadership that produces wealth for the organization. Knowing this helps to further justify the value in finding a perfect leader (wife).

This collection of 22 verses does not address the feminine characteristics of a wife, thus they have a greater interpretation for the area of leadership in general. The writer of this passage may not have downplayed the feminine characteristics on purpose, but rather simply emphasized other characteristics.

Relation to the Workplace

Proverbs 31:

> 12-14 "She brings him good, not harm, all the days of her life. She selects wool and flax and works with eager hands. She is like the merchant ships, bringing her food from afar."

> 16 "She considers a field and buys it; out of her earnings she plants a vineyard."

> 18 "She sees that her trading is profitable, and her lamp does not go out at night."

> 19 "She puts her hands to the distaff, and her hands hold the spindle"

> 21 "When it snows, she has no fear for her household; for all of them are clothed in scarlet, ..."

27 "She looks well to the ways of her household, and does not eat the bread of idleness."

We can better understand the perfect leader in relation to the workplace through verses 12-14, 16, 18, 19, 21, and 27. Verse 12 shows a leader who actively seeks the highest quality goods and services to use in the workplace, examining all potential services for best quality and price. The implication from this verse is that there is ample quantity to assure that other employees have plenty of material with which to work. This is not grudging work for the leader since the second part of verse 13 indicates that she works from a spirit of willingness, not of coercion (Cohen, 1946; Farmer, 1991; Plaut, 1961; & Ironside, 1908).

Verse 14 further demonstrates the resourcefulness of the leader (wife) by comparing her with merchant ships. Throughout the ages cultures have benefited from trading resources and goods not available in their local area. Likewise, a leader should go outside to discover new trends, ideas, and products to bring back to the organization, thus, emphasizing the importance of continuous improvement through training and development.

Verse 16 teaches us that the perfect leader considers buying assets that will expand the value of the organization (household). These wise purchases result in remaining funds. Within an organization, a leader strives to accomplish the same end result, spending less than budgeted and using the remainder to expand the value of the department. (This presumes that the more-senior leaders allow this behavior.)

Verse 16 defines the leader's role; she considers a field, which represents an idea that is barren without strategic plans. Then the leader purchases the field or *"buys into"* an idea and generates detailed plans to move the idea into reality. Then, with profit or remaining funds, (from a well-managed budget), the leader produces a vineyard that becomes fertile ground that yields fruit (more profit) in its season. This is similar to verse 24, which indicates that the perfect leader (wife) not only produces what the organization (household) needs, but also strives to produce an excess that she could sell in the marketplace for profit. She would then sow this increase back into the organization (Cohen, 1946; Farmer, 1991; Bridges, 1846; & Collins, 1980).

While the previous verses address the practical behavior of leaders, verses 18 and 19 refer to three traits of the perfect leader. The leader knows that what she does is good; she exhibits confidence in the work that she produces, and puts any spare time into industrious endeavors. Here the word "perceive" in Hebrew means, "to taste or eat" (Hamel, 1992). This implies a great responsibility to leaders who should believe and support their products or services to the extent that they themselves are willing to use them.

The latter part of verse 18 refers to the practice of keeping a lamp lit all night. Cohen (1946) refers to a Bedouin saying: "He sleeps in darkness" referring to a condition of poverty. Plaut (1961) takes a different view by commenting that keeping a lamp lit all night might indicate that the leader (wife) works long hours, or that she lives in a state of prosperity, for only the prosperous could afford to keep a lamp lit during the night. Regarding the parable of the Ten Virgins, this verse, as well as verse 21, indicates the practice of preparation. Leaders should have contingency or crisis plans to ensure the organization's welfare and productivity during unexpected or extraordinary events.

Verse 27 indicates that the perfect leader (wife) places the workplace first in need and desire. This character trait does not mean that the leader goes without important goods and services for herself. Several other verses imply that she profits from her labor. This indicates that the perfect leader (wife) knows who she is in relation to the workplace.

Relation to Self in the Workplace

Proverbs 31:

> 16 "She sets about her work vigorously; her arms are strong for her tasks."

> 20-22 "She opens her arms to the poor and extends her hands to the needy. When it snows she has no fear for her household for all of them are clothed in scarlet. She makes coverings for her bed; she is clothed in fine linen and purple."

> 25-26 "She is clothed with strength and dignity; she can laugh at the days to come. She speaks with wisdom, and faithful instruction is on her tongue."

> 30 - 31 "Charm is deceptive, and beauty is fleeting; but a woman who fears the Lord is to be praised. Give her the reward she has earned, and let her works bring her praise at the city gate."

Verses 17, 20-22, 25-26, and 30-31 provide insight as to how the perfect leader sees herself and relates to herself in the workplace. Verse 17 refers to the perfect leader (wife) girding her loins. Writers differ on the meaning of this. Collins (1980) says that this verse indicates that she is not adverse to moving beyond her femininity and getting dirty in her work. Hubbard (1989) refers to the use of the metaphor "girding," to describe the intensity with which she labors, for *"to gird the loins"* in Hebrew means to get to fight or to work hard. Cohen (1946) believes that she pulled her skirt up from the back and tucked it into her girdle (belt) to insure that her movements were unrestricted, allowing her to participate with the employees in hard work. Cohen's comment implies that the perfect leader (wife) is not afraid to engage in work that is usually handled by lower level employees. This is similar to the phrase *"rolling up your sleeves and joining the work."* We see a similar reference to women of status who willingly perform hard work in Genesis as when Rebekah willingly brought water to the travelers and to their camels.

The Proverbs 31 leader is not only humble and versatile enough to work alongside those of lesser rank in the organization, but, as verse 20 indicates, the perfect leader (wife) also meets the needs of the poor. This may imply the poor within or outside the organization. The perfect leader would not withhold resources from other departments that needed them, even if they could not afford them. In the Hebrew, we translate *"hand"* as *"open handed -- palm up."* This shows the liberality with which she gives to the poor (Cohen, 1946).

In this set of verses, the servant heart of the Proverbs 31 leader begins to unfold. Verses 21-22 show a relationship between the perfect leader (wife) and her employees. She provides for those whom she oversees before she provides for herself. McKane (1970) states that the reference to scarlet, fine linen, and purple demonstrates the leader's interest in quality.

By serving, the leader feels fulfilled, and as verse 25 demonstrates, the perfect leader (wife) finds self-esteem in her performance in the workplace. Cohen (1946) says that the reference to *"laughing at the time to come"* implies that she is quite comfortable with whatever may occur in the future because of her foresight in making provision. This preparedness improves her feeling of self-esteem and self-efficacy.

Verse 26 reveals that when the perfect leader (wife) speaks, her words are clear and full of wisdom. What she says shows kindness in her instruction (Alden, 1983). She does not participate in biting gossip or speak evil of anyone. Scripture has several references about women not speaking in public, similar to what many junior leaders must follow. This verse shows that when someone, like the perfect leader (wife), speaks with such wisdom and kindness, she is always welcome in conversation and finds many listeners.

Ironside (1980) reveals the secret of the perfect leader's success in verses 30-31. Her success and comfort is that she fears the Lord and holds Him in high esteem. Ironside goes on to say that although others may take pride in their beauty and winning words, the perfect leader rests in true character that comes from God. Hubbard (1989) helps us understand that the perfect leader (wife) relies on inner strength, not outward cosmetics that belie what is underneath the surface. Some leaders use charm or vanity to bluff their way up the corporate ladder.

A scriptural principle indicates that whatever one hides will not remain hidden, but will be exposed. In the long run, others discover that leaders who rely on these temporal qualities, lack the substance and genuine insight needed to effectively manage an organization. We do not cognitively learn this quality. It comes from the character developed in a relationship with God. It is this character that sets the stage for how the perfect leader relates to employees. It is noteworthy that the Book of Proverbs begins and ends with a reference to the importance of having a fear of the Lord (Farmer, 1991).

Relation to Employees in the Workplace

Proverbs 31:

15 "She gets up while it is still dark; she provides food for her family and portions for her servant girls."

21 "When it snows, she has no fear for her household; for all of them are clothed in scarlet."

27-29 "She watches over the affairs of her household and does not eat the bread of idleness. Her children arise and call her blessed; her husband also, and he praises her: 'Many women do noble things, but you surpass them all.'"

Verses 15, 21, 27, 28 give us some insight into how the perfect leader (wife) relates to employees. Verse 15 indicates that she arrives before other employees and prepares the workplace, if needed, so that all work can begin on time with the desired raw materials. The perfect leader ensures that all employees have what they need to do a good day's work. This implies both resources for the job and compensation for the day's labor.

The latter part of verse 21 and the first part of verse 27 indicate that the perfect leader (wife) provides only the best for her employees.

Because of what she does, verse 28 indicates that employees (the verse refers to children) regard her kindly. *"Her children rise up and call her blessed."* A positive relationship with employees results in employees thinking highly of her. This implies a probable willingness to work hard for her. The perfect leader (wife) should model this behavior in her relationships with her superiors.

Relation to Superiors in the Workplace

Proverbs 31:

10-12 "A wife of noble character who can find? She is worth far more than rubies. Her husband has full confidence in her and lacks nothing of value. She brings him good, not harm, all the days of her life."

23 "Her husband is respected at the city gate, where he takes his seat among the elders of the land."

29 *"Many women do noble things, but you surpass them all."*

Verses 10-12, 23, and 29 reveal the two-way relationship characteristics between the perfect leader (wife) and her superiors (husband). Verses 10 through 12 provide a statement of value, as recognized by the superior leader. Alden (1983) implies that the use of the word trust in verse 11 might imply that she inspires full confidence from those above her. Her superiors would repay this trust by giving her full control of what she did. The latter part of verse 11 says that the superior has *"no lack of gain."* Different writers offer different interpretations of this verse. Alden (1983) says that the superior has no unmet needs because of the efforts of the perfect leader (wife). Cohen says that the Hebrew word for *"gain"* implies the spoils of war, meaning that the superior gained what was not originally his. Bridges (1846) offers a different view by showing that the perfect leader (wife) provides so well that the superior (husband) has no need to go away from the organization (home) in order *"to enrich himself with the soldier's spoils"* (p. 621). These

159

interpretations show the perfect wife/leader as providing such an abundance that the superior has no unmet needs.

Verse 23 indicates that as a result of the perfect leader's work quality, the superior's peers highly regard him or her. The reference in this verse to the city gates implies that the superior is so confident in what the perfect leader (wife) does, that the superior can dedicate time to activities of a higher order.. This permits the organization to gain the most from both the perfect leader and her superior's labors.

Verse 29 shows the value of the perfect leader to the superior. The reference to daughters is a Hebrew language method of referring to all women rather than the literal "daughter" (Cohen, 1946). Valuing someone translates into rewards.

Relation to Rewards in the Workplace

Proverbs 31:

16 "She considers a field and buys it; out of her earnings she plants a vineyard."

22 "She makes coverings for her bed; she is clothed in fine linen and purple."

28-29 "Her children arise and call her blessed; her husband also, and he praises her: "Many women do noble things, but you surpass them all."

31 "Give her the reward she has earned, and let her works bring her praise at the city gate."

Verses 16, 22, 28-29, and 31 give insight as to the types of rewards that the perfect leader (wife) receives and how she handles them. Verse 16 indicates that the excess she generates is first put back into the organization to make it stronger. Verse 22 shows that she provides herself with the best only after the organization and her employees have what they need (Cohen, 1946; Bridges, 1846; & Alden, 1983).

Verses 28-29 indicate that both her subordinates and her superiors recognize her value and contribution and tell others how good she is. Verse 31 indicates that she gains praise from the marketplace. Earlier, verses 11 and 23 showed that the superior gained from the perfect leader. Now, in verse 31, the superior does what is necessary for the world to see who truly was responsible for the organization's well being. What a wonderful reward.

Conclusion

From these 22 verses we see the perfect leader as one who places the needs of others before her own, yet she is not ashamed to participate in the returns when there is excess for distribution. We see a leader who strives to perform so well that her peers esteem the superior because of her excellent work. We see a leader who considers the needs of the less fortunate in the organization and provides what she can to help them. We see a leader who is always willing to "roll up her sleeves" so to speak, to allow her to get in and work alongside her employees, without regard for the level of work at hand.

The driving force of this leader is that she has a fear of the Lord. She strives to do all that she can for her organization in order to make the organization and its employees the best that they can be. In summary, the Proverbs 31 leader:

Does good- v. 12

Seeks to find materials -v. 13

Willingly works-v. 13

Brings in valuable outside resources -v. 14

Rises early to work-v. 15

Provides for the workers-v. 15

Considers purchases, ideas, and solutions-v. 16

Girds with strength-v. 17

Perceives, believes in the organization-v. 18

Stretches out-v. 19

Holds (stability)-v. 19

Extends himself or herself -v. 20

Reaches out-v. 20

Is not afraid (unprepared)-v. 21

Makes (willing to roll-up his sleeves)-v. 22

Supplies- v. 24

Rejoices-v. 25

Speaks with wisdom-v. 26

Watches over the workers-v. 27

Doesn't partake in idleness-v. 27

FEARS THE LORD!-v. 30

Selah

If you would like to become a Proverbs 31 leader, consider which of these behaviors you currently exhibit and then strive to improve them. If there are behaviors listed here that you currently do not exhibit, begin now to change. It is never too late to begin to become a Proverbs 31 leader.

Chapter 13: Leadership and the Romans 12 Spiritual Gifts

Spiritual gifts in this essay mean the functional gifts found in Romans 12:6-8:

> *"We have different gifts, according to the grace given us. If a man's gift is prophesying, let him use it in proportion to his faith. If it is serving, let him serve; if it is teaching, let him teach; if it is encouraging, let him encourage; if it is contributing to the needs of others, let him give generously; if it is rulership, let him rule with diligence; if it is showing mercy, let him do it cheerfully."*

The term functional simply means that each gift has a different function, just as each member of the human body has a function. This same analogy carries over to the workplace. In our organizations, each person performs different functions in concert with other people to comprise the body of the organization. In contrast to the use of the term functional gifts, McRae defines spiritual gifts as talents rather than abilities. This is to say that some abilities may be gifts, but not all abilities are gifts. McRae states:

> Talents are also given by God to benefit mankind on a natural level, not spiritual. Like abilities they too should be dedicated to God to use for His glory. A spiritual gift is a divine endowment of a special ability for service upon a member of the body of Christ. A gift's source is divine. As to its essence, a spiritual gift is an ability. It is an ability to function effectively and significantly in a particular service as a member of Christ's body, the church. (p. 18)

Dr. Dorena DellaVecchio, in her research at the Regent University School of Leadership Studies, refers to the gifts as *"motivational gifts"* since the gifts represent the motivational drive for how a person should behave. DellaVecchio has developed a gift test that measures the presence of each of the Romans 12 Gifts. You may take this test on the worldwide web at http://www.gifttest.org. The test will give you a profile and a brief description of each gift.

The functional gifts as stated in Romans 12:6-8 include: (1) prophesying; (2) serving; (3) teaching; (4) encouraging; (5) giving; (6) ruling; and (7) mercy. Many writers substitute administering or leading for ruling (Selig & Arroyo, 1988; Weston, 1992; Mitchell, 1988; & Tooman, 1988), however, the Scriptures do not support this. *"Administration"* is listed in 1 Corinthians, but in a passage where the talents are categorized according to their importance within the church, they are not listed as gifts given to people. The term lead or leader did not emerge in the English language until after 400 A.D. and it is not found in the original Greek that is used to record Paul's letter to the Romans.

There have been many writers who claim that the Romans 12 gifts can only occur in Christians. Scripture does not support this and neither does the research conducted so far on spiritual gifts. Each of the three groups of gifts outlined in (a) Romans 12; (b) 1 Corinthians; and (c) the offices of the church that are recorded in Ephesians have distinct sources. Close examination of the original Greek shows that the Romans 12 passage refers to the gifts coming from God, while the 1 Corinthian gifts com from the Holy Spirit and the Ephesians' offices as assigned by Jesus. Research bears out the first claim, at least. We can give spiritual gifts tests to non-Christians (if the wording on the test is not biased toward the church) and they score such that it is clear they have certain gifts. However, when we give non-Christians a spiritual gifts test that focuses on the 1 Corinthians passage, they can't complete the exam.

According to Fortune and Fortune, everyone has a functional gift. They wrote, "[w]e tested tens of thousands of people and each one discovered his specific giftedness, falling under one of the seven categories, or sometimes under more than one" (p. 21). Fortune and Fortune believe: (1) that each person's gift was built into them when God formed them; (2) that this gift can be observed from childhood; (3) that this gift is to not be neglected, for to neglect it is to neglect God's purpose and plan for that person's life; (4) that this gift affects how the person views the world and circumstances around them; and (5) that this gift gives only one perspective of the whole. "God purposely limited and focused our giftedness so that we would work together and to remain dependent on each other in order to grasp the whole truth" (p. 25). Fortune and Fortune believe that everyone ministers in the spheres of all seven gifts, but that they function mainly in one primary motivational gift. They summarize their description of the gifts by describing a measure of whether someone operates in the sphere of his or her motivational gift. Someone in the sphere of the gift feels joy. "Joy is a by-product of operating within [the] motivational gift. Frustration is the by-product of operat[ing] outside it" (p. 37).

Fortune and Fortune's work with more than 100 groups and 1000 people over a 10-year period determined the following percentages of the population with the highest score in each gift:

Prophesying (see below where this is referred to as perceiving)	12%	Giver	6%
Serving	17%	Leader (see below where this is referred to as Ruler)	13%
Teacher	6%	Mercy	30%
Encourager	12%		

The Leader's Spiritual Gifts Profile: –
Putting All Seven To Work

In contrast to Fortune and Fortune work, my anecdotal research indicates that people have a profile of all seven spiritual gifts with some gifts being more dominant than others. The dominant gifts may be in line with Fortune and Fortune's work, but I think the profile gives a richer perspective and helps the leader better understand how to assign/allocate followers to different duties in the organization.

Consider any major leader who can be deemed as "a good leader" (this removes such leaders as Adolph Hitler and Genghis Khan), and you will find high amounts of each of the seven functional gifts. I have conducted an exercise with students in the United States as well as in South Africa over a three-year period and always get the same results. I begin the exercise with a Biblical leader such as David or Paul, and I ask students to tell me if the leader (David or Paul) had the "gift of perceiving" to which the majority answers, *"Yes."* I repeat this with each of the remaining gifts, and I get an affirmative answer to each question. I then ask the group of students for a leader from the country's past (in the United States I usually get Abraham Lincoln or Martin Luther King, Jr., and in South Africa, the students select Nelson Mandela). I repeat the process and get the same affirmative answer that the good leader is high in all seven gifts. What does this tell you about the gift profile of a leader? A good leader is high in all seven spiritual gifts. My anecdotal research so far, bears this out. Now, I just need to write the next book on leadership as a profile of the gifts to show all of the support that exists for this.

Perceiving

The gift of perceiving in Romans 12 is the most misrepresented of the seven functional gifts. Many authors believe that this gift in Romans 12 is the same gift of prophecy mentioned in 1 Corinthians 12. However, other authors define the Romans 12 gift of prophecy as the ability to quickly and accurately discern good and evil and the ability to reveal truth for understanding, correction, or edification. The key words here are correction and edification, which help distinguish this gift from the gift of teaching. The Greek word that we translate as *"perceiving"* is *propheteia*. It means *"revealing, manifesting, showing forth, making known, and divulging vital information."* The functional gift of prophecy in Romans 12 is the extraordinary ability to discern and proclaim truth.

Mitchell (1988) says that this gift is the giving of divinely inspired words that declare the purposes of God through three areas: (1) reproof, (2) comfort, and (3) revelation. The seven traits of a perceiver are: (1) the ability to spot a phony; (2) possession of strong opinions and dislike for compromise; (3) the need for outward evidence in someone's life to prove an inward heart change; (4) the enjoyment of lively debate, and the courage to stand alone; (5) the inner drive to communicate the truth of Scripture; (6) usage of a direct and frank approach; and (7) a desire to show people where their blind spots exist (p. 134).

DellaVecchio's work states that perceivers have a keen sense of right and wrong. My own observations support this, and I would add that the perceiver is compelled to tell the authority in the organization about the right and wrong that he or she comprehends. I advise leaders who have one or more perceivers working for them to keep the perceivers close at hand, listen to their advice, and act on the advice. I have observed perceivers who do not see the actions to correct the wrong or to protect the right becoming frustrated and begin to tell anyone who will listen about the problems they have seen. Whistle-blowers would usually score high in the gift of perceiving. Organizations don't need many perceivers (we probably couldn't survive many) but organizations need a few. Perceivers are particularly useful in audit situations, investigations, and quality control areas.

A study that would prove useful would be a study measuring the role of maturity in believers and how they use their functional gifts. Perceivers with low maturity can be brutal in their communication of the problems and can be seen as problem-employees. Perceivers with high maturity can be seen as wise counselors.

Serving

The gift of serving is the God-given ability to identify the unmet needs involved in a task and to make use of available labor-resources to meet those needs and to help accomplish the desired goals. This is not one-on-one, person-centered-like mercy but task-oriented. The Greek word for serving is *diakonia* and it means *"to aid."* People with the gift of serving are motivated to serve out of the enjoyment of helping. This motivation does not need outward recognition, but the server enjoys the recognition by others when the result is task completion. This means that people in your organization will help without being asked or compensated, but they will do better if the leader recognizes their extra contributions.

Selig and Arroyo believe that servers never seem to get excited or distraught about things, and that servers, often appreciated for their dry humor, tend to be uninvolved and prefer to be a spectator. Servers do not like change and change does not occur quickly when a person with the gift of serving is the leader.

Tooman believes that people with the gift of serving feel compelled to meet the practical needs of others. They feel driven to serve. Servers focus on tangible needs rather than spiritual ones. They enjoy short-range projects. They dislike red tape or any roadblock that prevents or hinders the successful completion of objectives.

Teaching

The gift of teaching is the God-given ability to clearly communicate the truths and applications of the Word in such a way that others will learn. The Greek word for teaching is *didaskalia,* which means to *"instruct, clarify, elucidate, illuminate, simplify, and to illustrate for the sake of communication and understanding."* People with the gift of teaching have the ability to discern, analyze, and deliver information and truth so that others will learn.

McRae states that teachers have a keen interest in studying and can communicate the truths and applications so that others may learn and profit. After one listens to a teacher, a typical response is, *"I see what he means."* Weston adds to the definition of the gift of teaching by saying that this is *"the supernatural functional gift that God gives to certain members in the Body of Christ which enables them to communicate information relevant to the health and ministry of the Body and its members in such a way that others learn"* (p. 63). Weston goes on to say that teachers present truth in a logical, systematic way, validating truth by research and by preferring the teaching of believers to engaging in evangelism. Teachers draw illustrations and applications from Biblical sources. Teachers emphasize accuracy at the expense of application.

Fortune and Fortune refer to teachers as the *"mind of the body."* Teachers always ask questions and need to know the truth, sometimes separate from the facts. Tooman expands the definition of a teacher by adding the characteristic of a driving urge to discover the truth. Teachers seek to know the details that alter the meaning of information and desire the proper use of words. They drive for accuracy and precision and desire it from others. Teachers find it acceptable to go for long periods of time without social interaction (p. 21).

Mitchell offers nine characteristics of the teacher: (1) loves research and checking information, words, and their definitions; (2) requires that words be used absolutely accurately; (3) finds it easy to gather, organize, and retain a large amount of facts; (4) is logical and is usually objective; (5) demands to know the authority behind information and insists that illustrations be completely within context; (6) implements an appropriate teaching method rather than giving a simple solution; (7) gives detailed instructions; (8) has a burning thirst for knowledge; and (9) searches for illustrations that add meaning to instructions.

DellaVecchio's work has revealed that teachers ask a lot of questions and sometimes appear to be antagonistic to leaders through the continuous search for the underlying logic of actions. Leaders need to be aware of when an employee with the gift of teaching is asking questions and realize that the employee is not questioning the logic of the leader, but is seeking to understand the logic so that the employee might fully embrace the project or request.

Encouraging

The gift of exhortation is a God-given ability to minister words of comfort, consolation, encouragement, and counsel in such a way that others feel helped and healed. Exhortation is from the Greek word *parakaleo* or *paraklesis*. The word has two parts: one is *"a call"* and the other is *"companionship."* Together they mean to be with and for another (Bryant, 1991). People with the gift of exhortation have the ability to call forth the best in others through encouragement and motivation.

Selig and Arroyo contrast teaching and exhortation by saying *"[w]hile the gift of teaching is like planting seeds, the gift of exhortation is like watering those seeds."* Tooman describes an exhorter as a person who is very personal, often charming. Exhorters act as a coach or mentor. They aspire to mold, shape, and motivate others. They possess a keen ability to see potential. Exhorters often provide a step-by-step process to those they encourage, so that those encouraged may reach the objective. Encouragers demonstrate a knack for determining exactly where a person is faltering. Exhorters are sociable and invigorated by personal interaction. They seek the rewards of warm relationships. Tooman finally adds a description of exhorters as positive and optimistic, tending to look forward to the future.

Giving

Tooman (1988) describes givers as people with a special talent for making and utilizing money. A person with this gift has a special visionary talent. Givers easily envision the results of their endeavors and possess a knack for making worthwhile investments. They are very frugal, often living below their income. Givers usually detect needs that others overlook. And they enjoy being included on the inner workings of organizations to which they give.

My observations are that givers don't need to give their own resources, but are quite good as stewards of other people's money. By this I mean you would find that someone with the gift of giving would perform very well in a philanthropic organization. Less dramatic, but equally important, you would find someone with the gift of giving working in budget allocation or supplies-disbursement. In either of these roles you would find givers making sure that people have the resources needed to do the job they are called to do. The key here is to see that givers focus on resources while servers focus on providing labor.

Ruling

The gift of rulership is the God-given ability to set goals in accordance with God's purpose for the future and to communicate those goals to others in a way that they harmoniously work together for the glory of God. The Greek word for leadership is *proistemi*, which means to stand over or place over, and is translated *"rule."* Many authors confuse this gift with leadership or with the reference to administration in 1 Corinthians 12. A careful read of 1 Corinthians 12 will show that administration is not a gift, but rather a place to apply the 1 Corinthians 12 gifts. The Greek that we translate into *"administration"* is closely aligned with "governance."

The focus on rulership here is on those in authority who carry out their duties quickly and with diligence (as the Greek is fully translated) DellaVecchio's research, supported by my observations, indicates that rulers have the ability to get the big picture, to see the plans necessary to accomplish the task, and to make decisions quickly. While rulers may make a mistake in their planning, new information will provide them with new data from which new plans emerge. The saying *"new information yields new strategies"* applies to rulers.

Selig and Arroyo (1986) provide eight characteristics of rulers: (1) executes projects and plans quickly; (2) are practical and forceful, with strong opinions on the best way to do things; (3) are prone to temper flare-ups when people do not meet expectations; (4) possess high ego strength; (5) are visionary by nature and easily get people excited about opportunities and challenges; (6) enjoy change and look forward to new challenges; (7) can be very domineering, may be impatient with people's inability to perform, and will push very hard; and (8) in confrontations, the ruler will attack first, often being very judgmental about a person's competence and ability.

Merciful

The gift of mercy is the God-given ability to feel genuine empathy and compassion for individuals, both Christian and non-Christian, who suffer distressing physical, mental, or emotional problems, and to translate that compassion into cheerfully done deeds (Wagner, 1979). The Greek word for mercy is *eleeo.* This translates as *"have compassion on."* People with the gift of mercy have the extraordinary ability to feel and to act upon genuine empathy for others who suffer distressing physical, mental, emotional, social, and spiritual pain (Bryant, 1991).

McRae describes those with the gift of mercy as giving undeserved aid directed toward the undeserving and those who are unable to repay. Those with the gift of mercy demonstrate sympathy, understanding, compassion, patience, and sensitivity toward the underprivileged. Those with the gift of mercy easily discern the motives of people, look for the good in people, and seek those who hurt, try to remove hurts and relieve distress, and easily detect insincerity in others.

Scriptural Gifts Applied to Leadership

Scripture is clear that the body is comprised of many parts, each with different skills and abilities. Paul's words do not directly state that the skills and abilities of the *"hand"* are not the same as the *"foot,"* but it can be inferred. At a particular time the *"hand"* may be the most prominent part, at other times the *"foot,"* but neither are the only parts of the body. For example, when building something out of wood, the *"hands"* may be more important than the *"feet."* When hiking, the *"feet"* may be more important than the *"hands."* It is the wise body that gives meaning and value to all the parts, but that allows one part to become more dominant than another given the circumstances. This is analogous to people in an organization, with you as a leader being the head. The head must constantly be aware of the needs, wants, desires, intentions, and environmental concerns of each part, including which elements to bring to the forefront.

When creating project teams, a leader should first look at the natural skills and abilities of prospective members (indicated by spiritual gift tests) before assigning functional responsibilities. For example, if you develop a new-product team, perhaps the spiritual gifts that you need apply to both marketing, as well as to production of the new product. Pick the team members so that the team possesses complimentary, as well as balanced functional and spiritual gifts. Thus, you create a team of marketing, production, finance, and logistics people as well as a team representing gifts of ruling, service, perceiving, teaching, etc., -- and it's all in one group of people..

Spiritual gifts are not the same as technical skills. Many leaders hire people for positions based on technical skills only to find, a few months later, that the employees are not working well in those positions. Let's use an example of secretaries. You may find someone with good skills in typing, filing, telephone, grammar and punctuation, and who answers all the right questions. Six months later, you discover that the individual is not as cooperative as you previously thought. In fact, co-workers complain that the individual does not get along well with others. In cases where this has occurred, leaders realized that the skills and abilities possessed in terms of technical skills were not sufficient to override the need for a gift of service. People with the gift of service tend to look beyond personality problems in order to get things done within the organization.

This raises a philosophical question. If everybody has different sets of spiritual gifts, how can we treat people equally when assigning job duties and responsibilities? The answer is that we can't treat them equally. We are not created equal. We are created with equal rights, as indicated by President Lincoln, and people have equal rights under the law, which is an issue of diversity in the workplace. Still, we must understand that people with particular skills and abilities should be given priority or better opportunity for certain assignments. You want to put the best people in the position that will best utilize their skills and gifts. This requires that we be just in our actions while not always being fair.

Selah

Have you taken the functional gifts profile at http://www.gifttest.org?

Are you balanced in your gifts?

Do you need to work on any areas that scored low?

If you scored low on all the gifts, you may be too hard on your self-evaluation. Ask someone who knows you well to take the test answering as they think you would and see what the results are.

Take time now to write down some of the steps you would like to take to develop your low gifts. Ask your employees for some ways that you might be stronger in the low gifts.

Chapter 14: Just Leadership – Not Fair Leadership

Nothing seems as difficult as interpreting the laws on discrimination and employee treatment. Scripture talks a lot about being fair and just. But, the concept of fair in the Bible is that of skin color or complexion, not treatment. It is not my intention to go against what the law says. What I do want to demonstrate is that Scripture states we must treat people justly. There may be different outcomes for different groups of people based upon what you offer them or based upon their skills and abilities.

For example, Scripture presents a parable where Jesus tells of a vineyard master who hired employees in the morning and at noontime. The vineyard master decided to pay both groups of employees the same day's wage. Those hired in the morning were frustrated because they felt they should receive more than those hired in the afternoon.

> *For the kingdom of heaven is like a landowner who went out early in the morning to hire men to work in his vineyard. He agreed to pay them a denarius for the day and sent them into his vineyard.*
>
> *About the third hour he went out and saw others standing in the marketplace doing nothing. He told them, "You also go and work in my vineyard, and I will pay you whatever is right." So they went.*
>
> *He went out again about the sixth hour and the ninth hour and did the same thing. About the eleventh hour he went out and found still others standing around. He asked them, "Why have you been standing here all day long doing nothing?"*

"Because no one has hired us," they answered.

He said to them, "You also go and work in my vineyard."

When evening came, the owner of the vineyard said to his foreman, "Call the workers and pay them their wages, beginning with the last ones hired and going on to the first."

The workers who were hired about the eleventh hour came and each received a denarius. So when those came who were hired first, they expected to receive more. But each one of them also received a denarius. When they received it, they began to grumble against the landowner. "These men who were hired last worked only one hour," they said, "and you have made them equal to us who have borne the burden of the work and the heat of the day."

But he answered one of them, "Friend, I am not being unfair to you. Didn't you agree to work for a denarius? Take your pay and go. I want to give the man who was hired last the same as I gave you. Don't I have the right to do what I want with my own money? Or are you envious because I am generous?"

Matthew 20:1-15 - NIV

Please note that although the New International Version uses the word unfair, all literal translations use the phrase *"do you no wrong."* The vineyard master believed it was just to pay both groups equally. This makes sense from the vineyard master's perspective if you examine the cost of living for one day. The daily minimum wage should equal the amount it takes to live for one day. The amount that the vineyard master paid each employee equaled the amount that it took to live for one day. My presumption with this parable is that those employees that were hired at noon were not slothful and hadn't just slept in missing the opportunity to work, but rather, the vineyard master decided at noon that he needed more workers and returned to the "hiring hall" to look for more able-bodied men. (See my earlier approach on this parable in the chapter on caring for employees.)

Christ also tells the story of a Gentile woman who approached Him wanting to receive the same blessing that He offered the Jewish people. Jesus explained that He was not supposed to do this, for He was sent to the Jews. The woman's response to Jesus was very wise and full of faith, and Jesus acknowledged and rewarded her great faith by answering her request.

> *A Canaanite woman from that vicinity came to him, crying out, "Lord, Son of David, have mercy on me! My daughter is suffering terribly from demon-possession."*
>
> *Jesus did not answer a word. So his disciples came to him and urged him, "Send her away, for she keeps crying out after us."*
>
> *He answered, "I was sent only to the lost sheep of Israel."*
>
> *The woman came and knelt before him. "Lord, help me!" she said.*
>
> *He replied, "It is not right to take the children's bread and toss it to their dogs."*
>
> *"Yes, Lord," she said, "but even the dogs eat the crumbs that fall from their masters' table."*

*Then Jesus answered, "Woman, you have great faith!
Your request is granted." And her daughter was healed
from that very hour.*

Matthew 15:21-28 - NIV

This parable provides an example of being just rather than
being fair. Is it fair that He gave her something that He did
not give to someone else? No, but fairness is not found often
in Scripture.

Unfortunately, we have a different situation in today's
organizations. We must give people equal assignments, equal
pay for equal work, and equal opportunity for advancement.
The intent of the original laws was to remove the barriers of
skin color, creed, national origin, and religion from
determining one's performance in the workplace.
Unfortunately, in many businesses we promote people to
positions that they are ill equipped to occupy because we
believe we must establish equality among groups of people.
Such a policy does a disservice to everyone involved.

I advocate placing people where their skills, abilities, and
spiritual gifts best match the requirements of the position.
This is where each person can best serve the organization.
People should be paid based on knowledge and capability,
not on years of service, rank, time, or grade. Instead, look at
what is just or what they deserve to have. This also ties into
discipline and mercy. We talk about discipline in terms of
doing what is just, not always doing what is equal or fair.

To help understand the concept of just versus fair, allow me
to recount an episode involving my three sons back in the
mid 1980s. Each of my sons is quite different with different
gifts, abilities, and callings on their lives. When they were all
small, the three of them were in the same room when one of

the boys asked me for something and I said *"No."* My son then looked at his brother and said, "But what about him, last week he got . . . " I responded that the prior week, each of the two boys got what they needed. The third chimed in that I had left him out, and I reminded the third of what he got in the prior week. The second son complained that the first son always got more. I was at the end of my patience and decided to teach the three of them a lesson about being fair and just. I responded that I liked him (the first son) best, to which the other two boys rose in unison to challenge my statement. I let the boys rant and rave a bit and then asked them if they really thought I liked one more than the others. The three of them calmed down and agreed that I liked them all equally.

Since the three boys were different, it was essential that I treat them differently and give them each what they needed (this is akin to the Platinum Rule mentioned earlier in this text). One son was very much interested in the military, so his mother and I had taken him and his friends to a military surplus store and paid for some military dress items so they could play in the nearby woods. Another son was very interested in sports, so his mother and I had recently paid for sports training. The other son was more interested in drama and acting, so we had supported his interest in a school play. I pointed out to the boys that to treat them equally would mean that they would all three have to be given the same thing -- but, only the one thing. The three boys quickly saw the loss of benefit for them to act collectively, especially if they had to be identical.

Like my sons, your employees are different and need different things. To treat them fairly requires that you treat them equally. To treat them justly requires that you give to each what each needs, and you expect from each what each can give.

To this day, the boys continue to tease me that each of them is my favorite, and I get cards and notes from "your favorite son" or "your best son" or something else along those lines. The boys remind me through humor that they know each has a relationship with me based on who they are individually and that they understand the value of being treated justly.

Selah

How is your leadership? Is it just? Or, are you trying to be fair?

Could your employees explain the difference? Or, could they recognize the difference?

If you are not sure if your employees could tell the difference, I encourage you to spend some time training on the differences.

Conclusion: How's Your Leadership?

Now that you are at the end of this work: How's your leadership? Do you measure up to the *agapao* standards, or are you like me and know that you aren't quite there yet? Do you wish to improve your leadership? If so, I encourage you to announce your commitment to improve to your employees and ask them to hold you accountable to the improvements. If your employees are like most employees, they want you to improve!

I also encourage you to spend time in prayer and ask God to show you the areas that you need to work on. Then I encourage you to get started improving! Don't worry if you fall back from time to time – get back on the improvement track and keep moving forward. *Agapao* leadership is as much a process of change for each of us as it is an end state that we seek.

As you improve – others will begin to ask you what is different in you – when this happens, show them the Sermon on the Mount, the Fruit of the Spirit, Proverbs 31 and the Romans 12 spiritual gifts and help the next person get started on the road to *agapao* leadership.

Blessings

--Bruce Winston, Ph.D.

References

Aitken, K. T. (1986). *Proverbs*. In Gibson, C. L. (Editor), *The Daily Study Bible (Old Testament)*. Philadelphia, PA: The Westminster Press.

Alden, R. L. (1983). *Proverbs: A Commentary on an Ancient Book of Timeless Advice*. Grand Rapids, MI: Baker Book House

Ansoff, H. I. (1988) *The New Corporate Strategy, Revised Edition*. New York: John Wiley and Sons

Augsburger, M. S. (1982). *Matthew*. In Ogilvie, D. (Editor), *The Communicator's Commentary*. Waco, TX: Word Books.

Baker, E. (1963). *The Neglected Factor - The Ethical Element in the Gospel*. New York: Abingdon Press.

Barclay, W. (1958). *The Gospel of Matthew - Vol I*. Philadelphia, PA: The Westminster Press.

Bauman, D. (1981). *Which Way to Happiness?* Ventura, CA: Regal Books.

Blanchard, K. and Bowles, S. (1993). *Raving Fans*. New York: Morrow.

Boice, J. M. (1972). *The Sermon on the Mount*. Grand Rapids, MI: Zondervan.

Bowman, J. W. and Tapp R. W. (1957). *The Gospel From the Mount: A New Translation and Interpretation of Matthew, Chapters 5 to 7*. Philadelphia, PA: The Westminster Press.

Bridges, C. (1846). *A Commentary on Proverbs*. Edinburgh, England: The Banner of Truth Trust.

Bryant, C. (1991). *Rediscovering our spiritual gifts.* Nashville, TN: Upper Room Books.

Cohen, A. (1946). *Proverbs.* London: The Soncino Press.

Collins, J. J. (1980). *Proverbs – Ecclesiastes.* Atlanta, GA: John Knox Press.

DePree, M. (1992) *Leadership Jazz: Composing Voice and Touch*, New York: Bantam Books

DellaVecchio, D. and Winston, B. (2002) "Validating a Motivational Gift Test for Secular Use." Working Paper, Virginia Beach, VA: School of Leadership Studies, Regent University.

Eddleman, H. L. (1955). *Teachings of Jesus in Matthew 5-7.* Nashville, TN: Convention Press.

Farmer, K. A. (1991). *Who Knows What is Good?* Grand Rapids, MI: Wm. B. Eerdmans Publishing Company.

Fortune, D. & Fortune, K. (1987). *Discover your God-given gifts.* Grand Rapids, MI: Chosen Books.

Fox, Emmet (1966). *The Sermon on the Mount.* San Francisco, CA: Harper.

Gibson C. L. (Editor) (1987) *The Daily Study Bible (Old Testament)*; Philadelphia: The Westminster Press.

Govett, R. (1984). *The Sermon on the Mount Expounded.* Miami Springs, FL: Conley Schoettle Publishing Co., Inc.

Hamel, K. (1992). *The Online Bible* (Macintosh Version 2.0) Oakhurst, NJ

Helgesen, S. (1995). *The Female Advantage: Women's Ways of Leadership.* New York: Currency/Doubleday.

Hersey, R. & Blanchard, K. H. (1982). Leadership of organizational behavior: Utilizing human resources (4th ed.). Englewood Cliffs, NJ: Prentice-Hall.

Hubbard, D. A. (1989). *Proverbs*. In Ogilvie, L. J. (Editor), *The Communicator's Commentary* Dallas, TX: Word Books.

Ironside, H. A. (1908). *Proverbs and the Song of Solomon.* Neptune, NJ: Loizeauzx Brothers.

Kissinger, W. (1975). *The Sermon on the Mount: A History of Interpretation and Bibliography.* Metuchen, NJ: The Scarecrow Press, Inc.

Lloyd-Jones, D. M. (1962). *Studies in the Sermon on the Mount.* London: Inter-Varsity Fellowship.

Martin, J. (1986). *The Sermon on the Mount.* Scottsdale, PA: Mennonite Publishing House.

McKane, W. (1970). *Proverbs: A New Approach.* London: SCM Press Ltd.

McRae, W. (1976). *The Dynamics of Spiritual Gifts.*, Grand Rapids, Michigan: Zondervan Publishing House.

Mitchell, M. L. (1988). *Giftedness: discovering your areas of strength.* Minneapolis, MN: Bethany House Publishers.

Palmer, E. F. (1986). *The Enormous Exception: Meeting Christ in the Sermon on the Mount.* Waco, TX: Word Books.

Pelikan, J. and Cardman, F. (1973). *The Preaching of Augustine.* Philadelphia, PA: Fortress Press.

Plaut, W. G. (1961). *Book of Proverbs: A Commentary*. New York: Union of American Hebrew Congregations.

Robertson, P. (1992). *The Secret Kingdom*. Nashville, TN: Thomas Nelson Publishers.

Rylaarsdam, J. C. (1964). *The Proverbs, Ecclesiastes and The Song of Solomon*. Richmond, VA: John Knox Press.

Selig, W. G. and Arroyo, A. (1988). *On Eagles Wings*. Virginia Beach, VA: Regent University.

Tooman, S. L. (1988). *INEX: A Self-Reporting Inventory Measuring Internal Motivations of an Individual and Their Subsequent Behaviors*. Virginia Beach, VA: Regent University.

Toy, C. H. (1904). *A Critical and Exegetical Commentary on the Book of Proverbs*. New York: Charles Scribner's Sons.

Wagner, P. (1979). *Your spiritual gifts can help your church grow*. Ventura CA: Regal Books.

Weisbord, M. R. (1991). *Productive Workplaces: Organizing and Managing for Dignity, Meaning, and Community*. San Francisco, CA: Jossey-Bass.

Weston, O. (1992). *Spiritual Gifts - Your Job Description from God*. Virginia Beach, VA: Regent University.

Winston, B. (1999). *The Master Leadership Builder and His Structure: A Story of Walls, Arches and Learning*. Virginia Beach, VA: Regent University School of Business Press.